THE SIXTH AMENDMENT

AN ILLUSTRATED HISTORY

ROBERT J. McWHIRTER

Copyright © 2017 by Robert J. McWhirter

All rights reserved. No part of this publication may be reproduced, distributed, or transmitted in any form or by any means, including photocopying, recording, or other electronic or mechanical methods, without the prior written permission of the publisher.

Published in the United States by Constitution Press
an imprint of RR&G Enterprises LLC
Post Office Box 26666
Tempe, Arizona 85285

Originally published in the United States as a chapter of
*Bills, Quills, and Stills; An Annotated, Illustrated,
and Illuminated History of the Bill of Rights.*

Distributed in the United States by Applewood Books
1 River Road
Carlisle, Massachusetts 01741
toll free: 800-277-5312
main: 781-271-0055

For bulk purchases for associations and other large groups,
please contact Applewood Books.

Library of Congress Control Number: 2017958119

ISBN: 978-1-945682-06-3

Design and layout of text by Quadrum Solutions

The Sixth Amendment

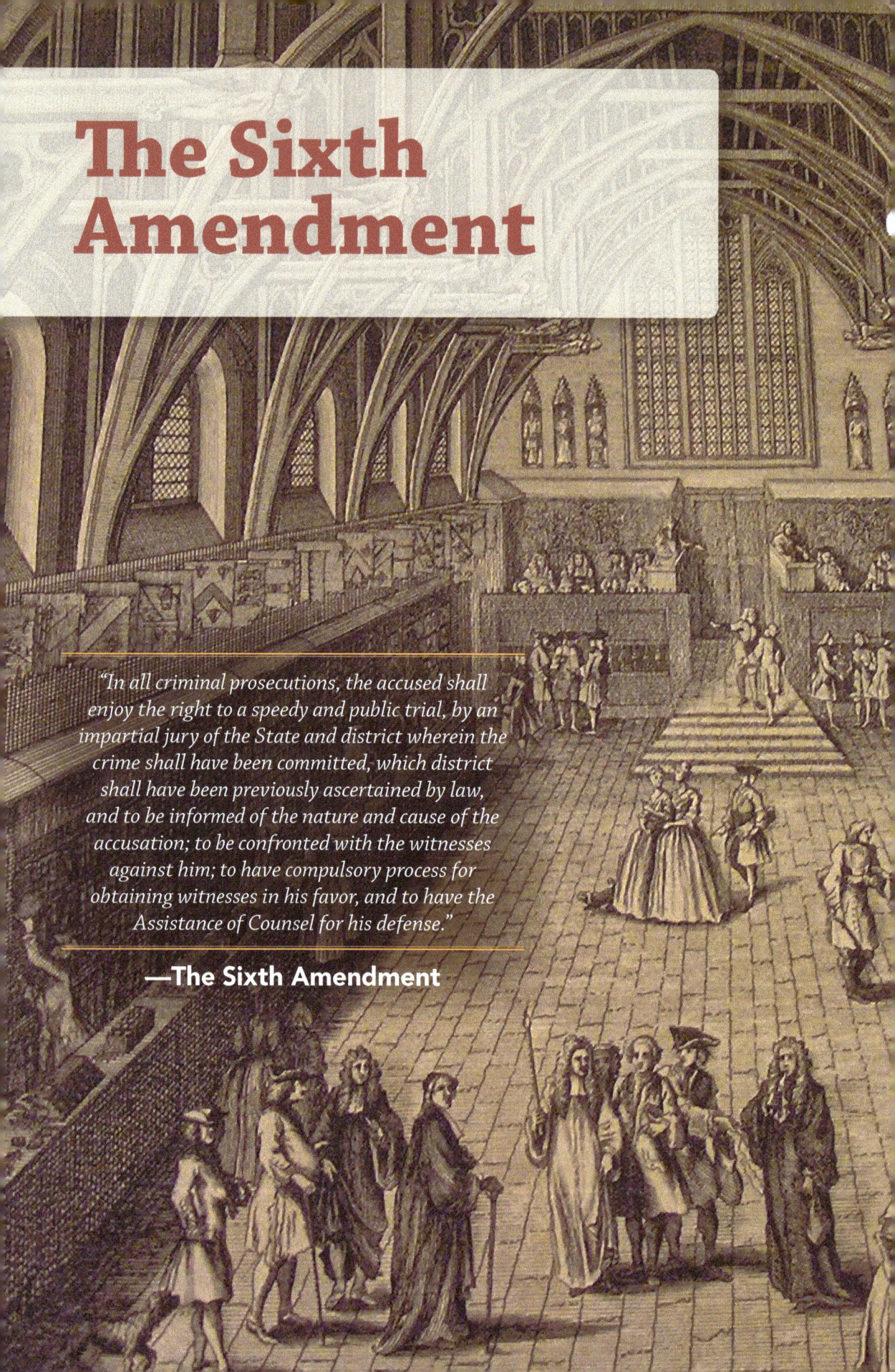

The Sixth Amendment

"In all criminal prosecutions, the accused shall enjoy the right to a speedy and public trial, by an impartial jury of the State and district wherein the crime shall have been committed, which district shall have been previously ascertained by law, and to be informed of the nature and cause of the accusation; to be confronted with the witnesses against him; to have compulsory process for obtaining witnesses in his favor, and to have the Assistance of Counsel for his defense."

—The Sixth Amendment

The Sixth Amendment ⟪ An Illustrated History

In 1649, John Lilburne needed to urinate.

He also needed a lawyer, notice of the charges, the right to subpoena witnesses, time to prepare his case, and the right to testify:

"I earnestly entreat you, that now you will pleased to give me a copy of my indictment, or so much of it, as you expect a plea from me upon, and an answer unto, and counsel assigned me, and time to debate with my counsel, and subpoena for witnesses."[1]

Lilburne got none of these rights. But, with persistence, he did get to pee:

"Sir, if you will be so cruel as not to give me leave to withdraw to ease and refresh my body, I pray you let me do it in the Court. Officer, I entreat you to help me to a chamber pot."[2]

1. 4 St. Tr. 1296, *quoted in* Harold W. Wolfram, *John Lilburne: Democracy's Pillar of Fire*, 3 Syracuse L. Rev. 213, 235 (1952).

John Lilburne, otherwise known as Freeborn John, was "[a]n honest and true-bred, free Englishman; that never in his life feared a Tyrant, nor loved an Appressor [sic]." Diane Parkin-Speer, *John Lilburne: A Revolutionary Interprets Statutes and Common Law Due Process*, 1 Law & Hist. Rev. 276, 296 (1983) (quoting William Haller & Godfrey Davies, The Leveller Tracts, 1647 to 1653, n.449 (1944). Another description was that Lilburne was "an obstreperous and forward opponent . . . constituted somewhere between a patriot and a demagogue . . . ." 8 John H. Wigmore, Evidence 291 (3d ed. 1940).

2. Wolfram at 245. A chamber pot is a bowl-shaped container, usually ceramic with lids, kept in the bedroom as a toilet, in common use until the nineteenth century. Webster's New International Dictionary of the English Language 446 (2d ed. 1942).

The chamber pot is the origin of the words "potty" and "potty training."

Contemplating the Zen of potty training

"[Whilst it was fetching, Mr. Lilburne followeth his papers and books close; and when the pot came, he made water, and gave it to the foreman.]"[1]

To be fair, judges had to complete trials in one sitting.[2]

But these judges had a special commission from Lord Protector Cromwell: kill Lilburne,[3] and Lilburne knew it.[4]

Lilburne's fight for his life helped us get the trial rights we take for granted. He laid the foundation for the list of trial rights that is the Sixth Amendment—the entitlements of the accused. Further, to make sure the accused gets all these rights, the Sixth Amendment finishes the list with the right *"to have the Assistance of Counsel for his defense."*[5]

"COUNSEL FOR HIS DEFENSE" IN HISTORY

Where there are courts, there are lawyers.[6]

Ancient Athenians defended themselves in court, but they could hire a *"logographos"* to write a speech for them to memorize.[7]

The Romans would appoint a *"procurator"* to handle legal business, especially when the party could not attend court. His function was like our modern attorney or agent for legal matters. Over time the Roman

---

1. Wolfram at 245 to 46.

2. Wolfram at 239 n.9. Not until 1794 did some criminal courts have the right to adjourn, that is, take a break.

3. Wolfram at 229. Cromwell issued an "extraordinary commission" of judges to get Lilburne's treason conviction, declaring that *"the Kingdome could never be settled so long as Lilburne was alive."* Quoted in LEONARD W. LEVY, ORIGINS OF THE FIFTH AMENDMENT: THE RIGHT AGAINST SELF-INCRIMINATION 300 (1968).

Oliver Cromwell

4. What Lilburne faced was like the "Double Secret Probation" that Dean Vernon Wormer put on Delta House in NATIONAL LAMPOON'S ANIMAL HOUSE (Universal Pictures 1978). So, from John Lilburne we get John Belushi!

Image by Helen Koop

5. U.S. CONST. amend. VI, cl. 3. The lawyer we all want to be is Atticus Finch from TO KILL A MOCKINGBIRD (Universal Pictures 1962), the film adaptation of Harper Lee's Pultzer Prize–winning novel (1960). Gregory Peck was tailor made for the role of a dignified Southern lawyer defending an innocent black man in the pre–civil rights South.

6. Regarding lawyers and the ancients, see R. BLAIN ANDRUS, LAWYER: A BRIEF 5,000 YEAR HISTORY (2009).

7. ROSCOE POUND, THE LAWYER FROM ANTIQUITY TO MODERN TIMES 32 (1953). "Logographos" derives from "logos" as in the modern "logo," like "team logo," but literally translated as "persuasive word" and "graphos," as in the modern "graph" or "graphic," but refers literally to "writing."

Socrates in his trial famously did not employ a *logographos*. THE WORKS OF PLATO, *Apology*, at 59 to 60 (Irwin Edman ed., Benjamin Jowett trans., Random House 1956).

8. POUND at 37.
Our word "attorney" comes from the Indo-European "*ter*," meaning "to turn," still seen in the English word "turn." The later Latin "*attorn*" meant "to turn over to another." The earliest attorneys were thus not necessarily lawyers but anyone designated to take the place of another in a transaction. We still see this when a person signs a "power of attorney" over to another who may be, but usually is not, an attorney. WEBSTER'S at 179.
Technically, an "attorney at law" is someone licensed to practice law, whereas a "lawyer" is someone "learned in the law" but not necessarily licensed. BLACK'S LAW DICTIONARY 118, 799 (5th ed. 1979).

9. POUND at 44 to 45.
For an example of the patron–client relationship, see Marlon Brando in Francis Ford Coppola's THE GODFATHER (Paramount Pictures 1972). The American Film Institute ranks THE GODFATHER No. 2 in its best movies list.

Empire's size made this more common.[8]

A Roman citizen who came to court to argue for others was a *"patronus causarum"* ("patron of the cause").[9] This term came from the great men of Rome, the patrons or patricians, who had many dependant client families and slaves. These were reciprocal relationships, and the patron would defend his "client" in court. Patrons who were good lawyers would get other people wanting to attach themselves to him to handle specific cases (or causes), hence *patronus causarum*. This is also the source of the modern reference of a lawyer "taking on a client."[10]

The Romans systematically taught rhetoric, and men like Cicero were great trial attorneys and cross-examiners.[11] Cicero defined "advocacy" as advancing

"points which look like the truth, even if they do not correspond with it exactly."[12]

Perhaps it was statements such as Cicero's that prompted Jesus, who was born just over a generation after Cicero, to say

"Woe unto you also, ye lawyers! For ye lade men with burdens grievous to be borne, and ye yourselves touch not the burden with one of your fingers."[13]

---

10. POUND at 46.

11. Cicero Denouncing Cataline by Cesare Maccari (1888).
  See C.A. Morrison, *Some Features of the Roman and the English Law of Evidence*, 33 TUL. L. REV. 577, 582 (1958). In the later empire, trials became inquisitorial and the art of cross-examination and other trial skills declined. *Id.* at 589; POUND at 50.
  Marcus Tullius Cicero (106–43 BC) was a Roman statesman, lawyer, political theorist, philosopher, and one of Rome's greatest orators and prose stylists. *Cicero*, OXFORD CLASSICAL DICTIONARY 234 to 38 (1970); COLUMBIA ENCYCLOPEDIA 558 to 59 (4th ed. 1975). Classical learning and history had great influence on America's Founding Fathers. *See, e.g.*, Louis J. Sirico, Jr., *The Federalist and the Lessons of Rome*, 75 MISS. L.J. 431 (2006).

12. *Quoted in* SADAKAT KADRI, THE TRIAL: A HISTORY, FROM SOCRATES TO O.J. SIMPSON 15 (2005).

13. *Luke* 11:46 (King James). For the trial of Jesus before the Sanhedrin, see J.W. EHRLICH, THE HOLY BIBLE AND THE LAW 146 (1962), noting that the Sanhedrin was the highest court of ancient Judea.

Just after Jesus's death, though, the Roman lawyer Quintilian wrote his text on rhetoric and cross-examination.[1] The Romans also gave us the first bar license and attempts to prohibit the unauthorized practice of law.[2] Because the lawyers were patrons, and thus leaders of great houses, they shunned getting paid as an advocate—at least officially. Emperor Claudius set the fee for lawyers at 10,000 *sesterces* or 100 *aurei*.[3]

In early medieval England, around the king's courts in Westminster, advocates began to congregate, working for a fee. Over two centuries after the Norman Conquest, Edward I issued an edict in 1292 directing the Court of Common Pleas to choose *"attorneys and learners"* to follow the courts and monopolize the legal profession.[4]

1. Pound at 48 to 49. **Marcus Fabius Quintilianus** (c. 35 to c. 100 AD) was a Roman rhetorician from Spain. Medieval and Renaissance schools of rhetoric widely used his writings. See http://www.thelatinlibrary.com/quintilian.html (last visited July 7, 2007) for a Latin text, and http://www.public.iastate.edu/~honeyl/quintilian/index.html (last visited July 7, 2007) for an English translation.

2. A law of 468 AD prohibited advocacy by those not admitted to practice in Roman courts. Pound at 51.

Saint Ives

3. This is about $475. Pound at 53. This 10,000 *sesterces* fee remained the standard, at least officially, throughout the Middle Ages. Saint Ives, canonized in 1347, was famous for being such a great lawyer that he always commanded the maximum fee, but so honest that he would accept no more. Thus depictions show him with the bag of exactly 10,000 *sesterces*. On his tomb was inscribed ("*Sanctus Ivo erat Brito / Advocatus et non latro / Res miranda populo*"). "St Ives was Breton / A lawyer and not a thief / Marvelous thing to the people." St. Ives Catholic Encyclopedia, http://www.newadvent.org/cathen/08256b.htm (last visited July 7, 2007). See *also* Pound at 5 to 54. Saint Ives is the patron saint of lawyers, not Saint Thomas More, who is the patron saint of statesman.

5. From the thirteenth century, the Inns of Court in London have been hostels and schools for training English lawyers. They were literally inns where students lived, ate, and learned. Today every English barrister belongs to an Inn, which supervises and disciplines its members, as well as providing libraries, dining facilities, and professional accommodation. Each also has a church or chapel. Over the centuries the number of active Inns of Court was reduced to four: Lincoln's Inn from 1422, Gray's Inn from 1569, Inner Temple from 1505, and Middle Temple from 1501. See A.W.B. Simpson, *The Early Constitution of the Inns of Court,* 28 Cambridge L.J. 241 (1970); Simpson at 241; Paul Brand, *Courtroom and Schoolroom: The Education of Lawyers in England Prior to 1400*, 60 Bull. Inst. of Hist. Research 147 (1987); S.E. Thorne, *The Early History of the Inns of Court with Special Reference to Gray's Inn*, Essays in English Legal History 137–54 (1985). Robert R. Pearce, A History of the Inns of Court and Chancery (1848).

Combined arms of the four Inns of Court

Roger More as Simon Templar in The Saint (1969)

Saint Thomas More

4. By the 1200, lawyers would hang out at Westminster and follow the court, cashing in on the fee-for-justice system. Danny Danziger & John Gillingham, 1215: The Year of Magna Carta 183 (2003); J.H. Baker, An Introduction to English Legal History 20 (2002); Colin Rhys Lovell, English Constitutional and Legal History 136 (1962).

The Middle and Inner Temple Inns get their name because they stand on the old English headquarters of the Knights Templar.

The Templars were the zealots yelling *"God wills it!"* in the movie Kingdom of Heaven (20th Century Fox 2005). Simon Templar, otherwise known as "The Saint," acts the modern day Knight Templar in Leslie Charteris's books, television show, and 1997 movie, The Saint (Paramount Pictures 1997).

This meant that unlike the rest of the English courts, and not the great universities, trained new lawyers. This led to the Inns of Court system.[5]

Because of the Inns of Court, English lawyers did not follow the pattern of the rest of Europe with lawyers trained in Roman and canon law.[6] Rather, English law became its own insular tradition, to which we in America are heirs.[7] A key part of that training, in addition to attending lectures and taking notes in court, involved the "moots" or practice arguments.[8]

Later we will talk more about lawyers, but we are ahead of the story. Lawyers need a place to practice law—and that place is a court.

---

6. BAKER at 28. For the outline of the medieval history of continental lawyers and their education in the great universities, see James A. Brundage, *The Medieval Advocate's Profession*, 6 LAW & HIST. REV. 439 (1988).

The Lawyers by Honoré Daumier (c. 1855), depicting lawyers from the Continental (i.e., non-English) tradition

7. Modern American lawyers are members of "the bar." The term comes from the Inns of Court, which, being inns, had bars. Later the bar was a railing that divided the hall in the Inns of Court, with students on one side and the readers or "benchers" on the other. Graduating students crossed the symbolic physical barrier and were "admitted to the bar." This is the origin of the word "barrister."

The drama of legal training formed the backdrop of John Jay Osborn, Jr.'s THE PAPER CHASE (1970) as well as *The Paper Chase* (20th Century Fox 1973) television show (CBS, 1978 to 79). The fictional Professor Charles Kingsfield uttered the now famous lines of clichéd pomposity, *"You teach yourselves the law. I train your minds. You come in here with a skull full of mush, and if you survive, you'll leave thinking like a lawyer."*

Professor Kingsfied – Image by Helen Koop

8. POUND at 89 to 90. By the end of the Middle Ages, the legal profession had three categories: (1) judges and serjeants, (2) apprentices in the Inns of Court, and (3) attorneys. *Id.* at 82. This is the origin of our modern notions of "lawyer" and "attorney."

The serjeants are what we today think of as courtroom lawyers, or the English "barrister," a lawyer who speaks for an accused. As early as 1259 the serjeants wore a coif, that is, a headdress. POUND at 81. But the modern wigs of English barristers and justices entered only with the Restoration, as part of French custom under Charles II. LOVELL at 151 n.26.

Conversely, an attorney is one who stands in for you as your agent. Anyone can give someone, not just a lawyer, a "power of attorney" to act in one's stead. *See generally* POUND at 77 to 93 ("Organization of Lawyers in Medieval England"); George C. Thomas III, *History's Lesson for the Right to Counsel*, 2004 U. ILL. L. REV. 543, 561 to 73 (2004) (noting historical distinction between pleaders as "sergeants" versus "attorneys" as agents); J.H. Baker, *Counsellors and Barristers: An Historical Study*, 27 CAMBRIDGE L.J. 205 (1969). England maintains the historical distinction between solicitors and barristers. Thomas at 572. The Sixth Amendment, however, more generally incorporates the "right to assistance of counsel," encompassing both functions.

The title "*serjeant-at-law*" comes from the Knights Templar whose senior Knights were "*freres sergens*" or "*fraters servientes*." KURT VON S. KYNELL, SAXON AND MEDIEVAL ANTECEDENTS OF THE ENGLISH COMMON LAW, 147–63 (2000).

The Order of the Coif is an honorary society for law students with good grades.

GOING COURTING

Where there are lawyers, there are courts.[1]

We "court."[2] A "suitor" goes "courting."[3] We can be "courteous," or a "courtesan," or just "curtsey"—all may be part of "courtship."[4] Dating is part of courtship, and, with a tennis date, we play on a "court."[5] If we play the game well, it "suits" us.

---

1. The U.S. Constitution provides for courts:

"The judicial Power of the United States, shall be vested in one supreme Court, and in such inferior Courts as the Congress may from time to time ordain and establish. The Judges, both of the supreme and inferior Courts, shall hold their Offices during good Behavior, and shall, at stated Times, receive for their Services a Compensation, which shall not be diminished during their Continuance in Office."

U.S. Const., art. III, § 1.

2. The word "court" comes from the Latin *"cohors,"* an enclosed farmyard (as in "horticulture" or as in a tennis or basketball court, or the modern word "cartilage" for a surrounding space or yard. Webster's at 611. The Latin word *"cohort"* for a tactical unit of one-tenth of a legion (one hundred men) in the Roman army passed into English to refer to any group of people (usually bonded by friendship). *Id.*

"Court," as a legal term, comes from *"cortem"* (Latin), *"cort"* (Old French), and *"curt"* (Anglo-Norman), combined with the word *"curia."*

At least one account of the connection between the court, as an enclosed yard, and a court as a place of law is that "court" referred to the inner courtyard of a castle. After the Norman Conquest, the castle courtyard was where the Anglo-Saxon commoners were allowed to call upon the local lord to settle disputes, hence the expression "going to court."

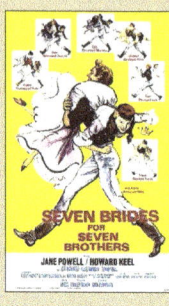

3. The verb "to court," as in "courtly love," is the basis of the words "courtesy," "courtesan," "curtsey" and the song *Going Courting* from Seven Brides for Seven Brothers (Metro-Goldwyn-Mayer 1954). Indeed, the term, "romance" and "romantic" come from the stories of courtly love written in the Latin vernacular of France, a Romance language (i.e., written in the language "of Rome"). See Webster's Word Histories 114, 400 to 01 (1989); John Ayto, Dictionary of Word Origins 141, 448 (1990).

4. Courtship is traditionally the wooing of a female by a male with dating, flowers, songs, chocolates, and other gifts. If a woman woos the man, she is a "suitoress." Scientists often compare the human activity of courtship with mating rituals of other animals. Today the term has an anachronistic quality compared to the more modern "hanging out" or "hooking up." American literary references include Henry Wadsworth Longfellow's The Courtship of Miles Standish (1858) as well as The Courtship of Eddie's Father (Metro-Goldwyn-Mayer 1963) and the TV spin–off (ABC 1969 to 72).

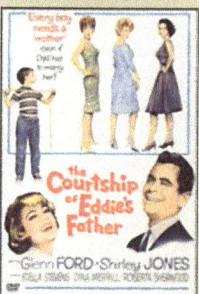

5. "Real tennis" is the original racquet sport from which modern tennis descends. The original game is closer to modern "court tennis" in the United States or "royal tennis" in the United Kingdom. The term "real" may be a corruption of "royal" and related to the game's connection with royalty in England and France in the sixteenth and seventeenth centuries.

Henry VIII was an avid tennis player and built several tennis courts, including one at his palace of Hampton Court, which is still the home to an active tennis club. Henry played there from 1528 until he got too fat.

A young, tennis-playing Henry VIII

A fat, non–tennis-playing Henry VIII

Hampton Court Palace

We go to court. In court, we argue as "suitors."[6] Our lawyers usually wear a "suit"—indeed, they are "suits."[7] A lawyer can assess his suit, which either means he is evaluating his case or looking at his clothes. He can also use a particular ability or fact and thus "play to his strong suit."[8] If he plays it wrong, he "courts" disaster.

From whence did all these courts and suitors come?

---

6. "Suitor" as far back as Anglo-Saxon times was a party in a dispute in the county courts (*shire moots*). BLACK'S LAW DICTIONARY 1286 (5th ed.). Today the word "suit" has several meanings, including a lawsuit, a business suit, swim suit, space suit, environmental suit, jumpsuit, etc. "Suit," comes from the Latin "*sequita*" and "*sequere*" and means "something that follows," as in the English "sequence," the root of the words "sect" and "set." It also referred to uniformed followers or retinue who wore the same suit. AYTO at 510. There is also "suite," as in a set or grouping in music or offices.

7. The suit as formalwear has gone through an evolution from the frock coat to the morning coat, which got its name for the fact that the coat's cut allowed gentlemen to get their morning exercise by horse riding. The morning coat was a more casual form of half-dress from the traditional frock coat. The once extremely casual "lounge suit" is now our business and formal suit. The slang "suit" to refer to professionals, establishment management, or government employees came first from Hollywood, referring to movie executives. Now artists, working people, and hackers use the term pejoratively for anyone in authority.

A "suit"

U.S. Department of Justice seal

A solicitor general's morning coat

◀ Stylized dudes from the 1920s, one with a double-breasted coat and the other sporting a morning coat

A formal frock, the morning suit or "cutaway," and President John Kennedy wearing the once very casual "lounge suit." The U.S. solicitor general and his assistants still wear the morning coat to argue before the Supreme Court. The movie TOMBSTONE (Hollywood Pictures 1993) has Kurt Russell's Wyatt Earp in a full frock coat, with Virgil and Morgan Earp in morning coats. Doc Holiday wears a "coachman's cloak," making it easier to hide the shotgun. In the movie MY COUSIN VINNY (20th Century Fox 1992), Vinny wears the "ridiculous" suit at the start of the trial but it is actually a more formal morning coat.

TOMBSTONE – Image by Helen Koop

8. A suit in cards is one of four categories dividing a deck: spades, diamonds, clubs, and hearts. Thus playing to your "strong suit" is playing your best cards.

THE ANGLO-SAXON COURTS

The Anglo-Saxon judges and ministers were *"witans,"* their courts *"moots,"* and their laws *"dooms."*[1]

For the Anglo-Saxons, justice was communal, a matter of custom, and connected with governance in general. The local court called the *"hundred"* met every month and dispensed justice to *"suitors."*

There were no lawyers or professional judges. Anglo-Saxon justice lacked executive power and was more akin to a modern arbitration. Indeed, at this time the "king's peace" was something special, an extension of the peace of his own house—i.e., his *"court"*—which only later became his courts.[2]

The *witans* were wise men, counselors, or ministers.[3] The *witan* met as the king's counselors in the *"Witenagemot"* (from *"witan"* and the Old English *"gemot,"* meaning "meeting" or "assembly").[4] *Gemot* is also the root word for *moot,* meaning an assembly or law court.[5]

The *Witenagemot* declared *dooms,* and the Anglo-Saxon county courts (*"shire moots"*) passed *"witena doms,"* which encompass our modern concepts of not just laws but also decrees, judgments, and statutes. The shire moots met twice a year.[6]

---

1. *See generally* BLACK'S at 909, 1436. Even before the Anglo-Saxons, Julius Caesar wrote of Celtic priest-judges called "druids" enforcing law and custom. BAKER at 2.

2. Sir Fredrick Pollock, *English Law Before the Norman Conquest,* 14 LAW Q. REV. 291, 292, 296, 301 (1898).

3. BAKER at 9. Our modern words *"wit"* and witness comes from the old English *"witan"* ("to know"). It is also the source of *"witless"*—destitute of wit or understanding; *"whittling"*—a person of little wit or understanding, a pretender to wit, one given to smart sayings but inferior in wit; *"witmonger"*—one who passes on smart or witty sayings; *"witship"*—a witty person; *"witsnapper"*—a maker of witty quips; *"witted"*—having wit or understanding; *"witticism"*—a witty saying, a sentence, or phrase, a clever or amusing expressed conceit formerly, a jeer or jibe; *"wittisize"*—to express oneself wittily or indulge in witticisms; *"witified"*—having wit; *"witting"*—knowledge, intelligence, judgment; *"wittingly"*—knowingly, knowledge of, by design; *"witty"*—possessed of wit; *"witwanton"*—using wit wantonly; *"wittooth"*—a wisdom tooth; *"witess"*—a female wit. WEBSTER'S at 2940, 2942.

WITNESS (Paramount Pictures 1985) stars Harrison Ford and Kelly McGillis, with the feature film debut of Viggo Mortensen. WITNESS FOR THE PROSECUTION (United Artists 1957) stars Tyrone Power, Marlene Dietrich, Charles Laughton, and Elsa Lanchester, and it is based on Agatha Christie's play about a master barrister defending a man for murder. When the defendant's wife unexpectedly appears for the prosecution, it tests the lawyer's skill to the limit.

Tyrone Power: WITNESS FOR THE PROSECUTION

4. George Jarvis Thompson, *The Development of the Anglo-American Judicial System,* 17 CORNELL L.Q. 9, 11 to 13 (1932) (hereafter Thompson I). R.C. VAN CAENEGEM, THE BIRTH OF THE ENGLISH COMMON LAW 13 (2d ed. 1988); A.K.R. KIRALFY, POTTER'S HISTORICAL INTRODUCTION TO ENGLISH LAW 11 (4th ed. 1958). See also Pollock at 292 n.2. Witans would have included senior clergy, the leading *"thegns,"* and *"ealdormen"* (from which we get our modern term "alderman"). All of the Anglo-Saxon kingdoms in England had a *Witenagemot*. At various times, especially in Wessex, the *witan* would elect the king. THE COLUMBIA ENCYCLOPEDIA 2996 (4th ed. 1963).

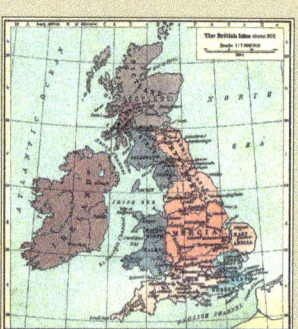
The British Isles circa 802

5. In various parts of England one can still find "moot halls" as meeting places, the remnant of the old *"folkmoot"* of the tribal Angles, Saxons, and Jutes. The Scandinavian people of Jämtland have the *"jamtamót"* or assmbly. As for modern references, the wizard court in the *Harry Potter* books and movies meets in the *"Wizengamot."* J. R. R. Tolkin's THE LORD OF THE RINGS' Ents meet in an *"Entmoot."* Tolkien was an expert in Old English literature and the epic BEOWULF.

Beowulf fights the dragon

A *doom* generally just meant an accounting or reckoning.[7] But it also implicated divine judgment or fate, and thus punishment from God, giving us our modern usage of the word.[8]

As a great council, the *Witenagemot* had what we would call today legislative and judicial functions.[9] As such it was the precursor of both Parliament and high courts. Thus, when Parliament tries a high public official or when the U.S. Senate tries a president or federal judge after the House of Representatives impeaches him, it exercises the function from its predecessor, the *Witenagemot*.[10]

Although the Normans replaced the *Witanagemot* with the *"Curia Regis,"* or King's court, the *moots* continued to function in the counties or, as the Anglo-Saxons would say, the *shires*.[11] They continued in the context of Norman law and custom as well as the king's emerging royal courts and an entire system of church courts that the Normans brought over with them to England.[12]

By 1278, the *moots* had lost all jurisdiction over criminal prosecution, but the courts limped on until 1846.[13] And as we noted, the Inns of Courts still use the word "moots" to refer to law school practice arguments. This history gives us the modern word and concept of something that new facts and events make "moot."[14]

---

6. Pollock at 292.

7. *The Doomsday Book*, William the Conqueror's survey of England in 1086, was an accounting of what England was worth. After William took over, he wanted to know the value of everything. In so doing, he gave history a window into the life of England at the time.

8. From Old English "*dōm*," Proto–Germanic "*domaz*," means "judgment," "law" (compare Sanskrit "*dhaman*," "law"). Webster's at 770.

Doom (id Software 1993) is a fun and gory first person "shooter" computer game invoking the modern understanding of the word.

9. See Pollock at 292. Regarding the powers of the *witan*, see Lovell at 15 to 16 (1962); Roscoe Pound, The Development of Constitutional Guarantees of Liberty 12 (1957) (noting that the "national council," which under Anglo-Saxon kings had been an assembly of wise men, became the Norman kings' court of his feudal vassals).

10. Thompson I at 13, *citing* the High Court of Parliament in England and the General Court of Massachusetts (consisting of the governor and both legislative houses) as examples.

A king and his *witan* from an eleventh century Old English hexateuch [British Library]

The 1999 U.S. Senate trial of President Bill Clinton after the House of Representatives impeached him

11. Baker at 6. The Shire is also the home of the Hobbits in J. R. R. Tolkien's fictional Middle-earth in The Lord of the Rings.
The word "*shire*" is still found in a great number of place and regional names in England and even in the state name New Hamp*shire*. New Hampshire was the ninth state to ratify the U.S. Constitution, the minimum number for it to take effect.

12. Van Caenegem at 12 to 13; *see also* Thompson I at 10 and n.3.

13. The County Court Act of 1846. *See also* The County Courts Amendment Act, ending the *hundred* courts. *Cited in* Thompson I at 13.

14. *See* Black's at 909.

THE NORMANS TAKE OVER

In 1066 AD, William the Bastard conquered England and thus became William the Conqueror.[1] (Getting your name changed for all of history from "the Bastard" to "the Conqueror" is at least one way to treat an inferiority complex.)

William did not replace the *Witenagemot*.[2] Rather, he rolled it into the *Curia Regis* but allowed the Anglo-Saxons to keep their laws, swearing upon his coronation to preserve *"the good ancient laws of the Anglo-Saxon kings."*[3]

William claimed his advisers were like the old *Witenagemot*, but in reality they were just a rubber stamp. He almost immediately sent his sheriffs to collect all the revenue they could get their hands on.

William brought to England feudalism: a system of social organization where everyone is a tenant to someone else, with the king being the ultimate landlord. William, however, accepted the concept that the king was *"first among equals" (primus inter pares)* among the barons.[4]

In this new mix of Anglo-Saxons, and Normans, the king became a unifying source of justice for both.[5] As time went on, more and more subjects would seek redress and justice from the king's

1. The Bayeux Tapestry depicting the Battle of Hastings.

2. Under the Anglo-Saxons, the *witan* elected, more or less, the king. When the *witan* "elected" William, it turned out to be its last act. LOVELL at 11.

3. KYNELL at 36; VAN CAENEGEM at 12; BAKER at 12.

4. LOVELL at 53, 60 to 61.

5. VAN CAENEGEM at 18.
This process began under the Anglo-Saxons, who believed that if *"the law was too heavy"* the king could give relief. POUND, DEVELOPMENT OF GUARANTEES, at 52.

6. In ancient Rome, a "*curia*" was a tribe or clan and came to mean the tribe's meeting place. The *Curia Romana*, or just the *Curia*, was the highest ecclesiastical court with jurisdiction over Europe, including England. *See* George Jarvis Thompson, *The Development of the Anglo-American Judicial System*, 17 CORNELL L.Q. 395, 399 (1932) (hereafter Thompson III). It is still the government of the Vatican State.

7. BAKER at 17. Thompson I at 18 n.49 (citing SIR WILLIAM S. HOLDSWORTH, HISTORY OF ENGLISH LAW 32 (3d ed.1922)) (noting that the *Curia Regis* was a feudal institution with membership based on land tenure, which the *Witenagemot* was not).
Over two centuries later, Edward I saw an advantage of bringing the new middle class into the *Curia Regis*. He called the Great Curiae in 1295 and 1305, which included many "common" knights and middle class. This was the beginning of Britain's House of Commons. Thompson I at 20. Edward I's *Curia Regis* moved from being just the king's advisers to the core of the later House of Lords. LOVELL at 132. For this reason his portrait hangs in the U.S. Congress.
Edward I was the king in the movie BRAVEHEART (Paramount Pictures 1995), played by Patrick McGoohan.

House of Commons

Edward I in U.S. House

"Norman" courts, rather than from the church, the local lord, or the old *shire moots*.

THE NORMAN COURTS

Norman courts start with the *Curia Regis,* or the King's Court.[6] William the Conqueror's successors developed the *Curia Regis* as a government institution.[7] Indeed, for centuries the entire government of England consisted of the "king in council," with authority delegated from him.[8]

With the many courts that existed in England (we today call these "forums"), church courts, manor courts, Anglo-Saxon *shire* and *hundreds* courts, the king's justice was sometimes hard to get.[9] This was especially true because his justice and court originally traveled with him.

Slowly, though, the idea that a court was something independent of the direct person of the king started to appear.

Although the *Curia Regis* would travel with the king over his dominions for centuries, William the Conqueror's son, King William Rufus, made Westminster Hall in London its center.[10] Thus a place existed where the courts and the common law would develop. Later, King Henry I started delegating judges to go to counties to hear pleas as if they were the king.[11] These judges were eventually called "*justiciae*" or "*justiciarius.*"[12]

---

8. Thompson I at 22. The judicial function of Parliament's House of Lords came from this part of the *Curia Regis*. Until the Constitutional Reform Act of 2005 and the new Supreme Court of the United Kingdom, the House of Lords was the U.K.'s court of last resort and the precursor of the U.S. Supreme Court. Historically, the House of Lords also functioned as a court of first instance for the trials of peers and for impeachment cases. This is the precedent for the American system where the Senate sits as a court for impeachment trials. Technically, the Lords sit as "the king in Council in Parliament," harkening back to the old role of the *Curia Regis* as being directly from the king's person. *See generally* Thompson III at 432 ("*[Lords] are vested with the entire judicial function of the High Court of Parliament . . .*"). *See also* FREDERICK G. KEMPIN, JR., HISTORICAL INTRODUCTION TO ANGLO-AMERICAN LAW 42 (3d ed. 1990).

9. The word "forum" comes from Roman trials. POUND at 44. Roman trials, *in judicio*, originally happened in the marketplace of Rome, called the "*forum,*" which later became the place of government and judicial proceedings. This is why we still call a court a forum to resolve legal questions, though today the statement tends to refer to jurisdiction or venue as in the statement, "this court is not the correct forum for this issue." Forum is also related to the Latin "*foris*" meaning "out of doors," which is where we get "forensic" as well as "forest." Later, Roman trials moved indoors to a large public building called a "*basilica.*" After the Roman Empire became Christian, the word "basilica" referred to a large and/or important church with special ceremonial status from the pope. Saint Peter's in Rome, for instance, is a basilica and not the cathedral of Rome.

A FUNNY THING HAPPENED ON THE WAY TO THE FORUM (United Artists 1966) starring Zero Mostel, from the stage musical with lyrics by Stephen Sondheim, is a comedic farce supposedly inspired by on the ancient Roman playwright Plautus. It is about Pseudolus, a bawdy slave who tries to win his freedom by helping his young master woo the girl next door.

Plautus (Titus Maccius Plautus (c. 254 to 184 BC))

Ruins of the Roman Forum

10. BAKER at 37; Thompson I at 19.

William Rufus (William II) was William the Conqueror's second son. The first son, Robert, got Normandy, the more valuable of dad's possessions. Henry, the next son, got squat from dad but by being smart and ruthless ended up with the whole realm. ANTONIA FRASER, THE LIVES OF THE KINGS AND QUEENS OF ENGLAND 27 to 31 (1975).

William Rufus (William II)   Henry I

11. VAN CAENEGEM at 20. These were "*curiales*" sent on "*eyres,*" "*itinera*" or journeys. *Eyres* is the root of our modern word "itinerary." BAKER at 16 n.15.

12. BAKER at 15. This gives us our modern title "justice," usually for the judges on a state or federal supreme court.

THE KING'S JUDGES

These traveling justices expanded the king's "court."

Although these justices had only the power the king delegated to them, for the first time a "court" became something more than attached to a person, as in "the king's court" where he "held court." (This could also be a bishop or baron's court.)[1] With the judges having the king's delegated authority to "hold court," the word "court" broadened to encompass our modern notion of a separate place for resolving legal disputes.

In 1166, a century after the Norman Conquest, King Henry II, William's great grandson, periodically sent *Curia Regis* judges to every county, taking over much of the work of the old Anglo-Saxon courts.[2] These judges had the king's commission under the great seal to supervise the justice system. Their job was to conduct an early form of investigative inquest called

---

1. LOVELL at 88.

2. In 1166, Henry II by statute transferred the jurisdiction from the shire courts to the king's courts. From 1154 to 1189, the shire courts also lost jurisdiction over land disputes. KEMPIN at 25.

3. BAKER at 17. The word "*oyer*" ("to hear") is related to the word "*oyez*" (pronounced "O, yez" and meaning "*hear ye*"; BLACK'S at 997). *Oyez* is the pronouncement many modern court bailiffs still use to commence a session such as the U.S. Supreme Court: "*Oyez!*

Oyez! Oyez! All persons having business before the Honorable, the Supreme Court of the United States, are admonished to draw near and give their attention, for the Court is now sitting. God save the United States and this Honorable Court!" "Oyez" is Law French, a form of Norman French that evolved over centuries in the English law courts. Town criers traditionally yelled "Oyez" to attract attention before a proclamation.

4. BAKER at 18; Thompson I at 24; Roger D. Groot, *The Jury in Private Criminal Prosecutions Before 1215*, 27 AM. J. LEGAL HIST. 113, 114

An assize judge riding circuit

(1983). The justices of the U.S. Supreme Court used to ride circuit and still have individual responsibility over the circuit courts of appeal. See David R. Stras, *Why Supreme Court Justices Should Ride Circuit Again*, 91 MINN. L. REV. 1710, 1711 (2007) (arguing that having justices return to circuit riding would help keep justices in tune with the country and help citizens know the court).

5. Thompson I at 25. The assize replaced the ancient *eyres*. The term "assize" comes from the Old French "*assises*" or "*sessions*" and is still the name of criminal courts in several countries, e.g., France, Belgium, and Italy. This is the source of the modern phrase, "*the court is now in session*." See WEBSTER'S at 612.

Westminster Hall on the first day of term, 1797

6. DANZIGER & GILLINGHAM at 179; BAKER at 13. Later, *Magna Carta* stated "*common pleas should not follow the king but should be held in some central place.*" *Id.* at 19 (citing *Magna Carta* 1215, cl. 17). See also A.E. DICK HOWARD, MAGNA CARTA: TEXT AND COMMENTARY 12 (1964). Westminster Hall continued for centuries housing, at various times, the Courts of Chancery, Common Pleas, King's Bench, and Exchequer. BAKER at 37.

"*oyer and terminer*" ("to hear and determine") or to try prisoners already charged with crimes, called "*gaol [jail] dilivery.*"[3]

King Henry II's court was "the bench" and eventually became the Court of Common Pleas. Judges of this central court in Westminster had responsibility for a circuit.[4] When the judges went out on circuit, they held an "assize."[5] They applied the same law and returned to Westminster to compare notes. Thus Henry II gets credit for starting the "common law."[6]

Forget our modern notion of judicial independence. Justices in medieval England were the king's men, well paid for implementing the king's justice.[7] Because any modern idea of police or prosecutors was centuries away,[8] these justices were, in part, de facto prosecutors and not the neutral referees we envision today.[9]

---

7. J.G. Bellamy, The Criminal Trial in Later Medieval England: Felony before the Courts from Edward I to the Sixteenth Century 10 to 11 (1998); Kempin at 88 to 91; Lovell at 110.

Not until the Act of Settlement of 1701 were the king's justices guaranteed secure salaries and life tenure. Kempin at 91 to 93; George Fisher, *The Jury's Rise as Lie Detector*, 107 Yale L.J. 575, 617 (1997). The U.S. Constitution protects judges in this regard at Article III, Section 1: "*The Judges, both of the supreme and inferior Courts, shall hold their Offices during good Behavior, and shall, at stated Times, receive for their Services a Compensation which shall not be diminished during their Continuance in Office.*"

8. But who knows what we think of as a judge after *Rowan & Martin's Laugh-In* classic skit with Flip Wilson, "*Here come da judge.*" Originally, British comic Roddy Maude-Roxby played a stuffy magistrate with black robe and powdered wig. The "judge" sketch would feature an unfortunate defendant brought before the court and guest star Flip Wilson introduced the sketch with "*Here come da judge!*" The catchphrase came from nightclub comedian Pigmeat Markham who later played the judge on the show. Later, Sammy Davis, Jr., donned the judicial robe and wig, adding such lines to the skit as "*If your lawyer's sleepin', better give him a nudge! Everybody look alive, 'cause here come da judge! Here come da judge!*"

Sammy Davis, Jr.

9. Forget *Law & Order*, where every program begins: "*In the criminal justice system, the people are represented by two separate yet equally important groups: the police, who investigate crime, and the district attorneys, who prosecute the offenders. These are their stories.*"
At this time there was no "criminal justice system," much less police or "district attorneys." *Law & Order* (NBC, from 1990 to 2010).

Rowan & Martin's Laugh-In (NBC, from January 22, 1968 to May 14, 1973) was an American sketch comedy television program that ran for 140 episodes. Comedians Dan Rowan and Dick Martin hosted it.

HENRY II GETS TOUGH ON CRIME!

Henry II also decided it was time to launch a "tough on crime" campaign.[1] The fact that getting tough on crime increased his power and revenues probably had nothing to do with it!

The nature of justice was changing. Since Anglo-Saxon times, justice had been a private matter but now was becoming a public concern. This was a slow process, spanning the reigns of several monarchs.[2] But the trend had begun, and Henry II played to it.

Getting tough on crime in twelfth century England meant challenging the church's jurisdiction. Before the Norman Conquest, England had no separate ecclesiastical courts or independent ecclesiastical law. The Norman kings created a dual system of courts and law.[3] Thus, in criminal matters, the church had a big chunk of jurisdiction that Henry II thought should be his.

Most of the early judges were clerics of one kind or another because generally only clerics could read or write.[4] Henry II began to change this. In 1179, he sent out twenty-one justices, most of whom were not churchmen and thus loyal only to him.[5]

Ten years later, in 1189, Henry introduced the Grand Assize, giving precedence to the king's courts over the local baronial courts. Thus the common law could develop into a universal system throughout the kingdom. Theoretically, under this system no one was above the law, not even the king.[6]

Motivating Henry was that justice was a moneymaker; enforcing criminal law meant

---

1. LOVELL at 101 (noting that under Henry II crime became a government matter). Henry was a busy guy. In addition to justice reform, he started the Plantagenet (aka Angevin) dynasty by becoming king of England, being duke of Normandy and count of Anjou, and marrying Eleanor of Aquitaine (by accounts a hottie with a big chunk of land). By his death, his dominions looked like the map shown here, and his relationship with Eleanor was scintillating enough for a movie, THE LION IN WINTER (Universal Pictures 1968).

2. *See generally* Daniel Klerman, *Was the Jury Ever Self-Informing?* 77 S. CAL. L. REV. 123, 130 to 32 and n.44 (2003 to 04), citing J.G. BELLAMY, THE CRIMINAL TRIAL IN LATER MEDIEVAL ENGLAND 103 (1998). In Europe getting tough on crime spurred the Inquisition. Richard M. Fraher, *The Theoretical Justification for the New Criminal Law of the High Middle Ages: "Rei Publicae Interest, Ne Crimina Remaneant Impunita,"* 1984 U. ILL. L. REV. 577 (1984). All of this was part of criminal law becoming a public concern rather than a private matter. *See also* Laura Ikins Stern, *Inquisition Procedure and Crime in Early Fifteenth-Century Florence*, 8 LAW & HIST. REV. 297 (1990).

The Ghent Altarpiece: The Just Judges (1427 to 30), showing Continental judges riding circuit

3. LEVY at 43. This was part of William the Conqueror's deal for the pope's blessing his English invasion. Under the Anglo-Saxons, bishops sat as judges. JOHN H. WIGMORE, EVIDENCE IN TRIALS AT COMMON LAW § 2250, 270 (McNaughton ed. 1961). For the split of king's and church courts, see Thompson III at 395 to 965, 400 to 02. *See also* Charles Donahue, Jr., *Ius Commune, Canon Law, and Common Law in England*, 66 TUL. L. REV. 1745 (1992).

4. KEMPIN at 89.

5. DANZIGER & GILLINGHAM at 179.
Regarding the power of early judges in Europe and England, see Walter Ullmann, *Medieval Principles of Evidence*, 62 LAW Q. REV. 77 (1946).

6. KYNELL at 52, 54.

fees, fines, and revenues for the enforcer. The king's judges collected more than enough revenue to both pay for themselves and to dump a lot into the king's coffers. Getting tough on crime was profitable, refuting the maxim that "crime doesn't pay"—it did for the king![7]

Regarding the church, Henry II's actions planted the seeds of a power struggle that was to play out over centuries.[8] This struggle involved the legal questions of what we today would call "subject matter jurisdiction" and "forum shopping."[9] As Henry knew, and modern lawyers know, the outcome of a case often depended on who heard it—the king, the archbishop, or the local baron.[10]

Henry's grant of primacy for the royal courts over the church courts stymied the growth of inquisitorial procedures in England. Thus Henry gets credit for England's developing the common law rather than inquisitorial procedure.

But English law did not develop independently from the rest of Europe. Both the church's and continental Europe's inquisitorial procedures influenced the common law.

The Inquisition always gets a bad rap. But the Latin *"inquisito"* actually translates as either "inquest" or the pejorative "inquisition." *Inquisito* originally meant nothing more than a judicial inquiry based upon a report.[11] In fact, many procedural protections now part of the common law actually came from the church's Inquisition—for example, the concept that a person is innocent until proven guilty.[12]

---

7. See BAKER at 502 to 03.
For example, coming back from the Third Crusade, King Richard the Lionheart was captured in Germany and held for ransom. His brother, John (later King John), used the law courts to raise the ransom. See KYNELL at 69.
In another example, justices from 1218 to 1219 raised £4,000 for King Edward I, who needed *"great treasure"* for the war on Scotland and raised it by *"causing justice to be done on malefactors."* Quoted in BAKER at 14. Thus, because justice was a moneymaker, Patrick McGoohan's Edward I got to beat up on Mel Gibson's William Wallace in BRAVEHEART.

8. During most of the medieval period, if a suspect made it to the church altar, he received sanctuary and a secular officer could not arrest him. KIRALFY at 363 to 64; BAKER at 512 to 13. Regarding *"criminous clerks"* and Henry II's struggle with Thomas Becket, see KYNELL at 56 to 58.

9. See generally Thompson III at 395 to 411 (the ecclesiastical courts); KIRALFY at 16 to 17; KEMPIN at 42.

Earliest known portrayal of Becket's murder

10. Henry II's assertion of royal jurisdiction brought him to his fateful conflict with Archbishop Thomas Becket. See also *The First Amendment, an Illustrated History*, in this series, published by Constitution Press. The English church/state power struggle did not resolve itself until Henry VIII effectively made himself Pope of England.

King Henry VIII

11. Walter Ullmann, *Some Medieval Principles of Criminal Procedure*, in JURISPRUDENCE IN THE MIDDLE AGES 1 (1980).

12. Kenneth Pennington, *Innocent until Proven Guilty: The Origins of a Legal Maxim* cited in PATRICIA M. DUGAN, THE PENAL PROCESS AND THE PROTECTION OF RIGHTS IN CANON LAW (2005); see also Walter Ullmann, *The Defense of the Accused in the Medieval Inquisition*, 481, 486 in LAW AND JURISDICTION IN THE MIDDLE AGES (George Garnett ed., 1988). See the discussion of the presumption of innocence later in this chapter.

The church also provided the concept that a person must intend to commit a crime before the act is a crime (i.e., a sin).¹ The common law eventually incorporated this as *mens rea,* or mental state.² This is why a child or an insane person who is unable to intend to commit a crime is innocent. This was a drastic change from the law before, which had provided that if a person was killed, it did not matter whether it was an accident or murder.³

Even in heresy trials, where the church relaxed many procedural protections,⁴ the accused still had an absolute right to his own advocate. The advocate was under oath to defend the accused fully under the law and to make any legal "exceptions" (i.e., objections).⁵ If the accused could not pay for his own lawyer, canon law allowed appointed counsel an honorarium from public funds.

Thus, under church law, a defendant would not have had to fight on his own.⁶ European criminal procedure, based in the *inquisito,* allowed for these procedural protections, including

---

1. Anselm, Archbishop of Canterbury in the 1090s wrote: "*Had they known it, they would never have crucified the Lord . . . a sin knowingly committed and a sin done ignorantly are so different that an evil . . . may be pardonable when done in ignorance.*" KADRI at 36 to 37.

2. For a general discussion of *mens rea* history, see Martin R. Gardner, *The* Mens Rea *Enigma: Observations on the Role of Motive in the Criminal Law Past and Present*, 1993 UTAH L. REV. 635.

3. Trial of Animals. Without a *mens rea* requirement, why not make an animal responsible for a criminal act? Even the Greeks prosecuted nonhuman killers such as dogs. PLATO, LAWS bk. IX (873D to 874A), *cited in* SADAKAT KADRI, THE TRIAL: A HISTORY, FROM SOCRATES TO O.J. SIMPSON 9, 146 to 77 (2005). During medieval times, animals got the right to confront their accusers and due process. Often this involved cases of sex with animals, i.e., buggery. Kadri recounts the interesting case of a Jacques Ferron in Vanvres, France, as late as 1750. The villagers came to court to testify as to the defendant's good character. Unfortunately for Ferron it was for the donkey, and he burned. *Id.* at 149 to 50. See a movie entitled THE ADVOCATE (European title: THE HOUR OF THE PIG) (1993) regarding the trial of a pig accused of killing a boy, set in fifteenth century France. Colin Firth represents the pig but more is involved than just the swine's culpability.

Execution of a sow

Underlying much of this was belief in witchcraft, because witches could always turn into animals. *See* **The Seventh Amendment**, in this series (briefly discussing witch trials). As for inanimate objects that kill, such as an axe, the law conceived of the "*deodand*" ("gift of God"). KADRI at 171. The object was forfeited to the king for distribution to the poor.

4. See *The Fifth Amendment, an illustrated history*, in this series, Constitution Press, 2017 for more on heresy trials.

5. Ullmann, *The Defense of the Accused*, at 482 to 83. The advocate did, however, have to promise to "desert" the cause as soon as he felt his position was irreconcilable with justice.

6. Counsel for the Defense by Honoré Daumier (c. 1860).

7. But in the end, even a lawyer is on his own, trial as Hamlet noted when looking at a lawyer's skull:

"*There's another: why may he be the skull of a lawyer? Where be his quiddits now, his quillets, his cases, his tenures, and his tricks? Why does he suffer this rude knave now to knock him about the sconce with a dirty shovel, and will not tell him of his action of battery?*" WILLIAM SHAKESPERE, HAMLET, act V, sc. 1.

"*Quiddits*" and "*quillets*" refer to hair-splitting arguments and trivial objections and relate to our more modern word "quibble."

A witch with her animals, casting a spell

Edwin Booth playing Hamlet. Booth was the most famous actor of his day but will be remembered as the brother of John Wilkes Booth

the right to a lawyer, centuries before the English common law.[7]

THE KING'S PEACE:

Most people wanted the king's peace, and they were willing to pay for it.

To get a case heard in the king's court, a person had to buy a "writ" (i.e., an order) from the king to his justices, directing them to hear the case, which was a considerable source of royal income.[8] And what the people got for their money were the king's professional judges, an inquest, and a jury of witnesses to find the facts, all backed up with royal muscle.

The people in fact demanded more of the king's peace from Henry II's fourth son, John, in *Magna Carta* Chapter 18. Generally, *Magna Carta* recognizes limits to the king's power, but this clause requires *more* rather than less of the king's power.[9] King John promised to send two justices to each county four times a year to hold assizes (or sessions).[10]

---

8. Thompson I at 22; Kiralfy at 21. For discussion of the writ system, see Baker at 54. A writ ("*breve*" in Latin and "*brief*" in French) was a thin parchment strip with a letter in the king's name sealed with the tip of the great seal. *Id.* at 57.

9. Danziger & Gillingham at 176 to 78. Baker at 20. Historians recognize King John's reign as a near total failure. He succeeded in losing nearly all dad Henry II's empire with the exception of England and the Channel Isles, winning him the nicknames Lackland (*Sans Terre* in French) and Soft Sword. No other English king or queen has since named their son John. For whatever reason, John was the first king to take the title *Rex Angliae* (King of England) instead of *Rex Anglorum* (King of the English). Lovell at 10 to 11.

King John is the bad guy in the Robin Hood movies, including Claude Rain's depiction in The Adventures of Robin Hood (Warner Brothers 1938), with Errol Flynn as Robin. Even Disney's animated Robin Hood (Buena Vista Pictures 1973) picks on King John, having him suck his thumb and cry for "*Mommy*" whenever Robin steals his gold, which is an amusing reference to his mother Eleanor of Aquitaine. He also says "*Mommy always liked Richard best*," a reference to his brother King Richard the Lionheart who no one would have dared called Soft Sword.

King John had to have had a serious inferiority complex. After all, his dad was the hyperactive, overachieving King Henry II, and his mom was Eleanor of Aquitaine, a ruler in her own right. John was a twerp who couldn't cut it.

But his weakness led to *Magna Carta*. As Winston Churchill wrote, "[w]hen the long tally is added, it will be seen that the British nation and the English-speaking world owe far more to the vices of John than to the labours of virtuous sovereigns." 1 Winston Churchill, A History of the English-Speaking Peoples, 190 (1958).

10. "*To no one will we sell, to no one will we deny or delay right or justice.*" *Magna Carta*, cl. 31, quoted in Danziger & Gillingham at 175; *see also* Howard at 15. Five of *Magna Carta*'s clauses limit a sheriff's powers (4, 24, 26, 30, and 48).

Winston Churchill

John's mom: Eleanor of Aquitaine

John's dad: Henry II

King John

Richard the Lionheart

King John

Katherine Hepburn and Peter O'Toole sparring as Eleanor and Henry in The Lion in Winter

John signs *Magna Carta*

It was "the *king's* peace," rather than just "the peace," because there were originally several "peaces" from which to choose.[1] The church or a local baron or lord offered peace within his own lands. *Magna Carta* shows the early stages of the "king's peace" growing from being one of several "peaces" in England to eventually the only one over the whole realm.

In America today, when a state or the federal government exercises its sovereignty (akin to the power of the sovereign king) to impose penalties under criminal law or civil regulation and uphold law and order, it imposes a type of king's peace. The English, in fact, still call it the king's (or queen's) peace.

Eventually, the "king's peace" arrived at a point where crime was not just against an individual victim but against the king's peace, *contra pacem regis,* and a personal affront to the sovereign. The English still caption a criminal case as *Rex (Regina) v. The Accused,* which in republics like the United States became *State, People,* or *Commonwealth v. The Accused.*[2]

If you had the king's writ, you could travel the realm and not be subject to anyone else's jurisdiction. School children, when playing a game, still shout for time out with "*Pax*" in England or "*King's X*" in America, reflecting this older notion.[3]

BRINGING THE KING'S PEACE WITH THE KING'S COURTS

Over time the king's courts expanded. As mentioned, a complete system of ecclesiastical courts already existed with very broad jurisdiction and ultimate appeal to Rome.[4] Courts also developed around the king's "*justiciar.*" Because the early Norman kings were often in France, the *justiciar* became a viceroy in the king's stead. As the kings spent more time in England—especially after John lost most of France—the *justiciar* became less necessary. After 1234

---

1. Justices of the peace used to be referred to as "justice of peace." Pollock at 184.

2. Lovell at 12; Baker at 60.

Elizabeth II presiding over the queen's peace

3. Lovell at 12. Modern English statute citation still recalls the king's role in establishing law and order through his peace. For example, the English statute "1 Eliz. II, cap.3" indicates the third law to receive royal assent during the first year of Queen Elizabeth II. *Id.* at 140.

4. Church courts had different procedures than the common-law courts with sworn testimony, proof by paper (sworn depositions), and pleadings. Lovell at 95.

The "*Roman Rota*" often heard these cases and exists today. Since the Middle Ages the case would go to "auditors" who would hear the evidence (Latin "*audire,*" "to hear or listen". The "*rota*" referred to the round table (Latin "*rota*") or the round room where they sat. Auditor, The Catholic Encyclopedia, http://www.newadvent.org/cathen/02070c.htm (last visited May 15, 2007). *See also* Baker at 126 to 27. The Roman Catholic Church's legal system is the oldest and one of the most advanced still in use today. In 1534 England abolished appeals to Rome. *Id.* at 130.

5. Baker at 15. Hugh le Despenser was a greedy man who wormed his way into Edward II's affections through a probable homosexual relationship. This did not sit well with Edward II's wife, Isabella, who eventually deposed Edward II. In a

Execution of Hugh Le Despenser

variation of the normal execution of traitors by hanging, drawing, and quartering, Hugh also had his penis and testicles cut off and burnt in front of him as punishment for his relationship with Edward.

Queen Isabella (also known as the She-Wolf of France) was by accounts as good looking as Sophie Marceau, who played her in Braveheart. *See* Alison Weir, Queen Isabella (2005).

6. See *The First Amendment, an illustrated history,* in this series, published by Constitution Press. regarding the office of chancellor.

justiciars were not regularly appointed and the last one, Hugh le Despenser, had a very bad end in 1265.[5]

With the abolition of the office of *justiciar,* much of his governing powers passed to the "chancellor," who became second to the monarch in dignity, power, and influence.[6] As for the *justiciar's* judicial powers, they were divided among what became the **Courts of Chancellery** and the three common-law courts of **Common Pleas, King's (or Queen's) Bench**, and **Exchequer**.

The **Courts of Chancellery** grew up around the chancellor, developing and applying the law of equity, often the great rival of the common law.[7] In chancellery court, if justice was on your side, you would win regardless of legal formalities, and the motto was *"nullus recedat a curia cancellariae sine remedio"* ("no one should leave the Chancery in despair").[8]

The **Court of Common Pleas** was the second oldest common-law court (after Exchequer), established during the late twelfth century. It generally dealt with civil cases between private parties. *Magna Carta* provided that there should be a court, the Common Bench (later the Court of Common Pleas) that met in a fixed place, Westminster Hall in London.[9]

The **Court of King's Bench** grew out of the king's court or *Curia Regis* and was not originally a law court but the center of the king's administration. Generally, its cases were criminal and civil cases where the government (i.e., the king) had an interest. It also supervised jurisdiction of all the courts by issuing writs of error, *mandamus*, and *certiorari*.[10]

The **Court of Exchequer** had by 1190 exercised a judicial role, with judges known as **barons**. Originally, this court dealt with actions by the crown for monies owed to it and actions by private citizens regarding financial matters with the king.[11]

Isabella and a young Edward III

7. Equity according to Aristotle was a way to correct general laws that could not cover every situation. It required decisions based on the law's intent rather than its wording. BAKER, at 106, citing ARISTOTLE, ETHICA NICOMACHEA, bk. 10 (W. David Ross trans., (Oxford Univ. Press, 1925).

8. BAKER at 102. Although equity grew to rival the common law, the Court of Chancellery worked in conjunction with the King's Bench. *Id.* at 101. Chancellery offered swift and inexpensive justice, especially for the poor, *id.* at 104, as opposed to the common-law courts that used an inflexible system of writs to do business. Writs were orders to the king's officials to take action. They were expensive and claims would fail just because a writ was incorrect. *See* George Jarvis Thompson, *The Development of the Anglo-American Judicial System*, 203, 209, *et seq.* (1932) (hereafter Thompson II); KEMPIN at 37 to 40. The king's chancellor could provide relief to injustice by issuing an injunction to stop the writ's execution. *See* Justin C. Barnes, *Lessons from England's "Great Guardian of Liberty": A Comparative Study of English and American Civil Juries*, 3 U. ST. THOMAS L. J. 345, 352 to 354 (2005). The Court of Chancery emerged soon after Edward I's death in 1307. LOVELL at 147.

9. *See* Thompson I at 36 to 38; KEMPIN at 33; BAKER at 44 to 47.

10. *See* Thompson I; at 38 to 41, KEMPIN at 34 to 35; G.R. ELTON, THE TUDOR CONSTITUTION (2d ed. 1982). See also BAKER at 41 to 44, 49 to 50.

11. *See* Thompson I at 35; BAKER at 47 to 49. Over time through legal fictions the Exchequer court's jurisdiction grew until, by 1290, it had become a regular common-law court on a par with King's Bench and Common Pleas. The Exchequer court got its name from the large table with squares. In ages before calculators and computers, or before Europe knew of the Chinese abacus, the table kept accounts straight by markers placed on the table to represent sums.

The squares, or check pattern, on the table also give us our term for "checks" as well as the game checkers and the terminology of chess ("check" and "checkmate") refer to the same type of table. BAKER at 18 and n.22; KEMPIN at 35 to 36. It was the Court of Exchequer that issued the writs of assistants that started the Boston writs cases, the precursor to the Fourth Amendment.

The jurisdiction between these courts waxed and waned over the centuries.[1] And there were other courts as well, exercising jurisdiction over subject matter or place.[2]

TUDOR AND STUART TRIALS

A defendant in Tudor England had the deck stacked against him.[3]

Trials during this time were unfair for the defendant because criminal procedure had changed greatly from the early system where jurors were the witnesses. The older system assured a form of rough community justice and balance. But this system had passed into history by Tudor times, and other procedural protections for the defendant had not yet developed.[4]

A defendant had no counsel, no evidence rules, no right to compel witnesses, and no right to see the indictment beforehand. The prosecution could interrogate him, sometimes under torture, because he had no protection against self-incrimination. The prosecution could present its case through summoned witnesses under oath.[5] Or, as we will see in the next section, the prosecution could present statements without having to even produce the witness because the defendant had no right to confront his accusers.

Although the defendant had a public trial by jury,[6] he was not informed of the charges against him until the day of

---

1. For a description of the original jurisdiction of the courts, see BAKER at 38. In 1880, the various courts were reorganized with Common Pleas, the King's (then the Queen's) Bench, and Chancellery combined into the High Court of Justice. The jurisdiction of American courts has from the start included all the common-law subjects as well as equity. See Thompson I at 42. Regarding early colonial courts, see KEMPIN at 44 to 47. Today most U.S. courts are courts of law and equity. See FED. R. CIV. P. 2 (1938).

Four illuminations on vellum from around 1460 showing the four courts at Westminster Hall—Chancery, Common Pleas, King's Bench, and Exchequer. They are part of the Inner Temple Library's collections and provide the earliest known depictions of the English courts and court dress. Inner Temple Library, http://www.innertemplelibrary.org.uk/welcome.htm (last visited May 15, 2007).

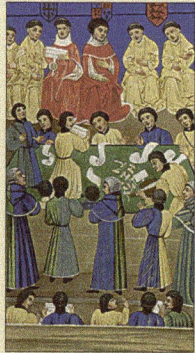
Court of Chancellery

Court of King's Bench

Court of Common Pleas   Court of Exchequer

As one scholar has stated, "[t]he most distinctive feature of the emergent criminal trial in Tudor England (1485 to 1603) was the imbalance of advantage between the state and the accused." Peter Westen, *The Compulsory Process Clause*, 73 MICH. L. REV. 71, 81 (1974).

2. Other courts included Admiralty, Thompson III at 414, and the Courts of the Lord High Constable and Earl Marshal of England, *id.* at 421 to 24 (the latter was charged with marshalling the king's forces and is where we get the modern term "court marshal," which also is spelled "court-martial," showing the association with the military). *See also* BAKER at 122 to 24. There were also the king's prerogative courts such as the Star Chamber and the High Commission. *See* Thompson II at 203 to 29; KEMPIN at 40 to 41; BAKER at 117 to 19. The abuses in these courts helped bring about the English Revolution and their abolition. Thompson II at 240 to 43; KEMPIN at 75. Finally, the House of Lords, as part of the High Court of Parliament, is the precursor to the U.S. Supreme Court. Thompson III at 432; KEMPIN at 42.

3. The Tudors: Henry VII, Henry VIII, Edward VI

Mary, and Elizabeth

trial. He thus had no time or right to collect his own evidence or witnesses.

A defendant could make a statement in his defense but not under oath.[7] He lived or died depending on what he said. An "altercation" is how Sir Thomas Smith, a scholar and official of Queen Elizabeth I, described the trial.[8]

The altercation began as soon as the defendant pleaded not guilty and the sheriff called the local jury. Although the defendant could challenge a juror if he had cause, this rarely happened. The jury was sworn and began to hear evidence, usually from a justice of the peace who read to the court and jury his written record of the defendant's and witnesses' statements. If there were live witnesses, only the judge interrogated them.[9]

After this altercation, the judge told the jury what he thought of the evidence and how they should vote. The jury would probably hear several cases and then deliberate. The whole trial lasted less than an hour; a model of brevity and efficiency. To top it off, there was no appeal—they could convict and hang you the same day.

But criminal procedure was starting to change, and men were fighting for the right to defend themselves.[10] Sir Walter Raleigh argued for the right to confront his accuser. He didn't get it, but because of him, we do.

---

4. *"In short, while changes were under way that would soon transform the criminal trial into a truly adversary proceeding, criminal trials in the sixteenth century were primarily one-sided inquests into the truth of the prosecution's charges."* Westen at 82.

5. Westen at 82.

6. Westen at 82.

7. Westen at 84 argues convincingly that *"the rule arose at a time when the jurors themselves were considered the sole 'witnesses' to the facts, and simply failed to adjust to reflect the new role of the jury as a trier of evidence presented by others."*

8. **Sir Thomas Smith** (1513 to 77), an English scholar and diplomat, was one of Elizabeth's most trusted Protestant counselors, appointed in 1572 as chancellor of the Order of the Garter and a secretary of state. Smith's book, *De Republica Anglorum—the Manner of Government or Policie of the Realme of England*, was written between 1562 and 1565, and published in 1583. See http://www.constitution.org/eng/repang.htm (last visited May 31, 2007). See Stephan Landsman, *The Rise of the Contentious Spirit: Adversary Procedure in Eighteenth Century England*, 75 Cornell L. Rev. 497, 504 to 05 (1990) (summarizing Smith's description).

The most prolific modern scholar on this subject, John Langbein, coined the phrase *"the accused speaks"* model of trial, which describes the main aspect of trial—the defendant's statement. *See, e.g.*, John Langbein, *The Criminal Trial before the Lawyers*, 45 U. Chi. L. Rev. 263 (1978) I, however, have chosen to use Smith's phrase of the *"altercation"* trial because it better describes the courtroom dynamic and because Smith wrote before Langbein.

9. See Landsman, *Contentious Spirit*, at 513 to 14, describing judicial interrogation from the inquisitorial model. Tudor and Stuart trials were *"nasty, brutish, and essentially short."* Id. at 498 (quoting J. S. Cockburn, A History of the English Assizes 1558 to 1714, at 109 (1972)).

10. Sir Nicholas Throckmorton's treason trial of 1554 lasted one day from 7:00 a.m. to 5:00 p.m. *See generally* P.R. Glazebrook, *The Making of English Criminal Law: The Reign of Mary Tudor*, 1977 Crim. L. Rev. 582, 586 to 88. He had no lawyer, no time to prepare, no right to call witnesses. The judges and prosecution engaged in *"one continuous onslaught on the defendant."* Id. at 587; Fisher at 603. But he stood his ground, defended himself well, and the jury acquitted him. The judges were so angry they sent the jurors to prison! (Judges could do this until 1670.) The Supreme Court referred to Throckmorton in *Miranda v. Arizona*, 384 U.S. 436, 443 (1966). Throckmorton was imprisoned, released, and fled to France but by 1557 was back in favor with Queen Mary and later rose rapidly in the service of Queen Elizabeth. His daughter Elizabeth married Sir Walter Raleigh. London's Throgmorton Street is named for him.

SIR WALTER RALEIGH AND THE HISTORY OF THE CONFRONTATION CLAUSE

The right to confront your accusers is over two thousand years old, coming

"to us on faded parchment, . . . with a lineage that traces back to the beginnings of Western legal culture."[1]

As William Shakespeare knew, it is dramatic:

King Richard: *"Then call them to our presence, face to face and frowning brow to brow, ourselves will hear the accuser and the accused freely speak."*[2]

The essence of cross-examination is the right to confront any witness. Thus, from Vinny to Kaffee, it's a Hollywood mainstay![3]

As we will see, despite history and Shakespeare, Sir Walter Raleigh in 1603 didn't get the right to confront.[4]

---

1. *Coy v. Iowa*, 487 U. S. 1012, 1015 (1988). See Fred O. Smith, Jr., *Crawford's Aftershock: Aligning the Regulation of Nontestimonial Hearsay with the History and Purposes of the Confrontation Clause*, 60 STAN. L. REV. 1497, 1506 (2008).

2. WILLIAM SHAKESPEARE, RICHARD II, act 1, sc. 1, *quoted in Coy* 487 U.S. at 1014. *See also* DANIEL J. KORNSTEIN, KILL ALL THE LAWYERS?: SHAKESPEARE'S LEGAL APPEAL 194 (1994) (citing RICHARD II at act 1, sc. 1, ll. 15 to 17); *see also* Graham at 213 (citing *Richard II* and *Much Ado About Nothing*).

  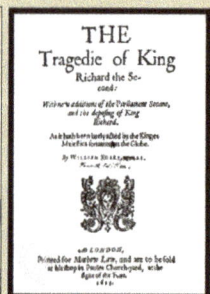

Richard II

3. Movies like MY COUSIN VINNY and A FEW GOOD MEN depend on the dramatic value of confrontation through cross-examination.

MY COUSIN VINNY (20th Century Fox 1992) Image by Helen Koop

4. *Crawford v. Washington*, 541 U.S. 36, 44 to 45 (2004) provides a standard history. *But see* Thomas Davis, *What Did the Framers Know, and When Did They Know It? Fictional Originalism in Crawford v. Washington*, 71 BROOK. L. REV. 105 (2005); Robert Kry, *Confrontation under the Marian Statutes: A Response to Professor Davies*, 72 BROOK. L. REV. 493 (2007).

Regarding the leading historical theories on the Confrontation Clause, see Daniel Shaviro, *The Confrontation Clause Today in Light of Its Common Law Background*, 26 VAL. U. L. REV. 337 (1991).

A FEW GOOD MEN (Columbia Pictures 1992) Image by Helen Koop

Confronting with the Greeks and Romans:

Socrates argued during his 499 BC trial about the lack of confrontation:

"And the hardest of all, I do not know and cannot tell the names of my accusers . . . for I cannot have them up here, and cross-examine them; and therefore I must simply fight with shadows in my own defense, and argue when there is no one who answers."[5]

Socrates's "shadow boxing" in his own defense remains one of the best metaphors for the right to confront your accusers.

Although "confrontation" is a modern legal term, the concept is old, with Romans requiring proceedings *viva voce* ("live voiced").[6]

The Catholic Church later incorporated the Roman rule in canon law.[7] Indeed, at times the church could be extremely technical about its application.[8] Part of the reason for the church's exactitude, though, was the Bible.

---

5. THE WORKS OF PLATO, *Apology* 60 (Irwin Edman ed., Benjamin Jowett trans., Random House 1956). An Athenian trial consisted of the parties making a speech during which they called and cross-examined witnesses. POUND at 33.

Socrates

6. As the Supreme Court noted: "[s]imply as a matter of Latin the word "confront" ultimately derives from the prefix "con-" (from "contra" meaning "against" or "opposed") and the noun "frons" (forehead)." *Crawford v. Washington*, 541 U.S. 36, 44 to 45 (2004).

Emperor Hadrian

Pope Gregory I

7. Frank R. Herrmann & Brownlow M. Speer, *Facing the Accuser: Ancient and Medieval Precursors of the Confrontation Clause*, 34 VA. J. INT'L. 481, 511 (1994). For example, the Emperor Hadrian while sitting as a judge rejected written testimony against an accused. *Id.* at 489. Justinian's Code later incorporated this rule assuming that the witness will testify before the adverse party. *Id.* at 490 to 93. Pope Gregory I (also known as Pope Gregory the Great) adopted this rule for the Catholic Church, *Id.* at 493–99, which remained the rule until excepted for heresy prosecutions. *Id.* at 535 to 37.

8. The Cadaver Synod. Pope Stephen VI hated his predecessor Pope Formosus so much he put his dead body on trial in February 897 AD. But because Formosus still had the right to confrontation, they unsealed his vault at Saint Peter's and brought his eight-month-old corpse to court. KADRI at 160. They put him in papal robes, condemned him, hacked off the three fingers of his right hand he used for blessings, and had him buried in a potter's field. Grave robbers dug him up but found nothing valuable and threw him into the Tiber River. *Id.* at 160 to 61. Later Stephen was dethroned and strangled in prison, and his successor Theodore II rehabilitated poor Formosus. A monk "miraculously" found the body after a year and a half out of the grave and ten months in the Tiber. His "body" got a new set of papal robes and a third reburial.

Despite the right of confrontation, the church from then on prohibited any future trials of dead bodies.

Pope Formosus and Stephen VII (now Stephen VI) by Laurens (1870)

Confronting in the Bible: Susanna was a hottie of biblical proportions.[1]

Two old guys saw her in the garden and wanted sex. If she didn't, they would say they saw her commit adultery. (How's that for psychological projection!)[2]

What was she to do?

Susanna stayed virtuous and true, so the scorned elders accused her of adultery.

At trial, the prophet Daniel volunteered as her lawyer and saved her by confronting the accusers:

"Daniel said to them, 'Separate these men and keep them at a distance from each other, and I will examine them.'"

Daniel showed their accusations to be inconsistent.[3]

Because Susanna got a lawyer and the right of confrontation, virtue triumphed and she was acquitted.[4]

As the Susanna story shows, the right of confrontation provided a check to keep oaths and testimony valid, a key biblical theme:

"With his mouth the godless destroys his neighbor, but through knowledge the righteous escape."[5]

The right of confrontation gave Daniel the knowledge to let *"the righteous escape."* As the Ninth Commandment states:

"Thou shalt not bear false witness against thy neighbor."[6]

Indeed,

"the thief is better than a man that is accustomed to lie."[7]

And to guarantee truth, the Bible prescribed questioning and confrontation:

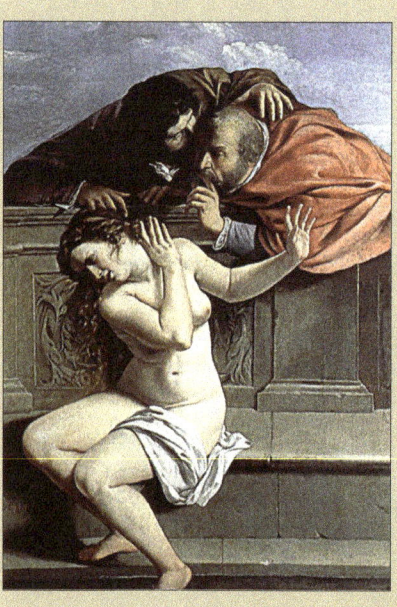

1. *Susanna and the Elders* by Artemisia Gentileschi (**1610**).
For a nice account of this story identifying Daniel as an early "public defender," see ANDRUS at 35 to 41.

4. Virtue triumphed every week for Perry Mason but without the right to confrontation you get no Perry Mason. The key to every case was Perry's (actor Raymond Burr's) incisive cross-examination of the real bad guy (or sometimes gal) who breaks down on the witness stand. Of course, Perry did one better than Daniel and actually got the bad guys to admit guilt on the stand.

Perry Mason ran on radio from 1943 to 1955 and on television from September 1957 to May 1966. There were later television versions with Raymond Burr reprising the role. The title character is a fictional Los Angeles defense attorney who originally appeared in detective fiction by Erle Stanley Gardner.

Matlock (NBC, from September 23, 1986, to May 8, 1992) had basically the same confrontation formula as *Perry Mason* but with Andy Griffith providing a homespun quality.

2. *Susanna* 1:164. Protestants consider this story of Susanna as apocryphal, but Catholics and Eastern Orthodox Scholars include the story in the Book of Daniel as Chapter 13.

3. *Susanna* 1:52 to 59. The two old guys diverged as to what type of tree under which they saw Susanna fornicating; one said a mastic and the other an evergreen oak.

Raymond Burr

"And the judges shall make diligent inquisition: and, behold, if the witness be a false witness, and hath testified falsely against his brother, then shall ye do unto him, as he had thought to have done unto his brother . . . ."[8]

Jesus had a variation on the confrontation and adultery theme.

Jesus's enemies brought a woman before him accused of adultery.[9] The penalty would have been her death by stoning.[10] The real issue, though, was that they wanted to catch Jesus condoning disobedience to the law by showing compassion. But using the right of confrontation, he avoided the problem with a legal nicety:

"Hath no man condemned thee? Neither do I condemn thee: go and avoid this sin."[11]

Because no one was around to confront, and perhaps implicate himself, Jesus beat his enemies at their own game.[12]

Later Saint Paul stood accused before the Roman governor Festus and demanded his right as a Roman citizen to confront his accusers:

"To whom I answered, that it is not the manner of the Romans for favor to deliver any man to the death before he which is accused, have the accusers before him, and have place to defend himself, concerning the crime."[13]

When King James I charged Sir Walter Raleigh with high treason in 1603, Raleigh could rely on Socrates, the Romans, Susanna, and Saint Paul to demand and plead for the right to confront his accuser.

Daniel, from Michelangelo's Sistine ceiling

5. *Proverbs* 11:9. Regarding oaths in the ancient world.

6. *Exodus* 20:16.

7. *Ecclesiastics* 20:25; EHRLICH at 199.

8. *Deuteronomy* 19:18, 19; EHRLICH at 172. For the penalty for false witness, see *Deuteronomy* 19:18.

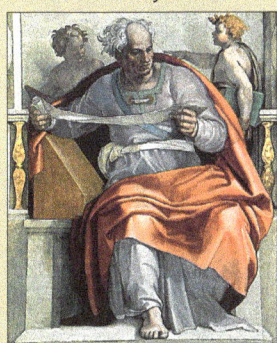

Old Testament prophet/judge Joel, from the Sistine ceiling

9. *Christ and the Woman Taken in Adultery* (1621).

10. See *The Eighth Amendment, an illustrated history*, in this series, published by Constitution Press, 2017.

11. *John* 8:3 to 7.

12. *See* Kenneth Graham, *Confrontation Stories: Raleigh on the Mayflower*, 3 OHIO ST. J. CRIM. L. 209, 214 (2005) (criticizing Justice Scalia's view of history and arguing that the right to confrontation was not in the common law but in the colonies from the Puritan's reading of the Bible, such as the woman taken in adultery without an accuser).

13. *See Coy v. Iowa*, 487 U.S. 1012 (1988) (quoting this passage from *Acts* 25:16).

Saint-Paul before Governor Festus

Festus was one of Matt Dillon's deputies and a sidekick in the television show *Gunsmoke*, which originated on radio (1952 to 61) and ran on TV from 1955 to 1975.

Confronting with Sir Walter Raleigh: Raleigh was a poet, courtier, explorer,[1] and one of Queen Elizabeth I's favorites.[2] He looked good in a good-looking court. But Elizabeth's successor, James I, didn't like him at all.

In November 1603, James had him tried for treason, charging him with conspiring with Lord Cobham and others on behalf of Spain. The basis of the charge was pure hearsay: a sailor named Dyer testified that *"someone in Lisbon"* told him that James would never be king because Raleigh and Cobham would slit his throat.[3]

At one point in the trial, Raleigh let loose:

"Do you bring the words of these hellish spiders against me? . . . I find not myself touched, scarce named; and the course of proof is strange; if witnesses are to speak by relation to one another, by this means you may have any man's life in a week; and I may be massacred by mere hearsay."[4]

But upon interrogation (and perhaps torture) in the Tower of London, Cobham implicated Raleigh.[5]

Although Cobham later recanted, at Raleigh's trial the prosecution read his statements to the jury. Every man, Raleigh insisted, had the right to confront his accuser.

Cobham, Raleigh logically argued, lied to save himself:

"Cobham is absolutely in the King's mercy; to excuse me cannot avail him; by accusing me he may hope for favour."[6]

Raleigh called for his common-law right to confront his accuser:

"The Proof of the Common Law is by witness and jury: let Cobham be here, let him speak it. Call my accuser before my face . . . ."[7]

---

1. Sir Walter Raleigh (1552 or 1554 to 1618) established the first, though unsuccessful, English colony in America (June 4, 1584) at Roanoke Island, North Carolina. Raleigh counties in North Carolina and West Virginia, among other places, are named for him.

2. Raleigh is the guy who laid his cloak before Elizabeth's feet (one of the great suck-up feats in history!). His relationship with Elizabeth I is the subject of numerous depictions, including the movie THE VIRGIN QUEEN (20th Century Fox 1955) (Bette Davis and Richard Todd) and ELIZABETH: THE GOLDEN AGE (2008) (Clive Owen and Cate Blanchett), a sequel to ELIZABETH (Gramercy 1998). Elizabeth was called the Virgin Queen because she never married, probably to keep power, and is not a comment on her chastity. *See, e.g.,* CHRISTOPHER HIBBERT, THE VIRGIN QUEEN: ELIZABETH I, GENIUS OF THE GOLDEN AGE (1992).

Bette Davis as Elizabeth

King James I.

Sir Edward Coke, the prosecutor, argued this hearsay was good evidence, responding in court to Raleigh, *"Your treason had wings."*[8]

The judges refused his request, though Raleigh persisted; after all, even in trial by ordeal, the accused had the right to confront his accuser. But Raleigh's was truly an altercation with Attorney General Coke:

Coke: *Thou art the most vile and execrable traitor that ever lived.*

Raleigh: *You speak indiscreetly, barbarously and uncivilly.*

Coke: *I want[i.e., lack]words sufficient to express thy viperous treason.*

Raleigh: *I think you want words indeed, for you have spoken one thing half a dozen times.*

Coke: *Thou art an odious fellow, thy name is hateful to all the realm of England for thy pride.*

Raleigh: *It will go near to prove a measuring cast between you and me, Mr. Attorney.*[9]

Coke at the end of his case decided on a bit of showmanship. He pulled out of his pocket another Cobham letter, once again confessing the plot with Raleigh and retracting his retractions with *"nothing but the truth . . . the whole truth before God and his angels."*

Matching the showmanship, Raleigh then pulled out from his pocket yet another Cobham letter exonerating Raleigh: *"I never practiced with Spain by your procurement; God so comfort me in this for my affliction, as you are a true subject, for any thing that I know . . . God have mercy upon my soul, as I know no treason by you."*[10]

Although Cobham probably wrote this "last" letter before Coke's, Raleigh got the last word.

---

3. KADRI at 83.

4. *Quoted in* KADRI at 83.

5. KADRI at 82.

6. *Crawford*, 541 U.S. at 44 (citing D. JARDINE, CRIMINAL TRIALS 435 (1832)). For an excerpt from CRIMINAL TRIALS 389 to 520 (David Jardine ed., 1850), see http://www.wfu.edu/~chesner/Evidence/Linked%20Files/Additional%20Assigned%20Readings/TRIAL%20OF%20SIR%20WALTER%20RALEIGH.htm (last visited June 3, 2007).

7. Cobham.

8. KADRI at 82.

9. Many consider Coke's conduct during this trial a blemish on his strong record in the development of the common law and judging. While on the King's Bench he stood against King James I at his life's peril. Perhaps, though, his conduct during the trial was not out of line for its day. For the quotations of Raleigh's cross-examination from the *State Trials*, see Allen D. Boyer, *The Trial of Sir Walter Ralegh: The Law of Treason, The Trial of Treason and the Origins of the Confrontation Clause*, 74 MISS. L.J. 869, 892 to 93 (2005).

10. Boyer at 893. Raleigh had contacted Cobham to get this "last" letter by putting a note in a hollowed out apple, which he threw in Cobham's cell. Given Cobham's numerous contradictory statements, he would have easily been impeached under today's Federal Rule of Evidence 801(d)(1).

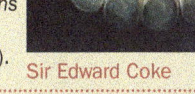
Sir Edward Coke

Sir Walter Raleigh

In the end Raleigh never got the right to confront his accuser. And despite Raleigh's protestations that his trial was "*the Spanish Inquisition,*" the jury convicted him and the court gave him the death sentence.[1]

By any standard, the procedure in Raleigh's trial was unfair. As one of Raleigh's judges lamented, "*the justice of England has never been so degraded and injured as by the condemnation of Sir Walter Raleigh.*"[2]

But his trial led to various legal reforms guaranteeing the right to confrontation, such as the requirement in treason law of a face-to-face confrontation. Courts also created rules of unavailability, admitting out-of-court statements only if the witness could not testify in person. Courts also ruled that a suspect's statements could only incriminate himself, not another.[3] These reforms became part of the common law, which over 150 years later gave the context for the Sixth Amendment's Confrontation Clause.[4]

Despite these reforms, however, the altercation criminal trial was slow to change.[5]

LILBURNE STILL PLEADS FOR A LAWYER

And now we're back to John Lilburne needing to pee.

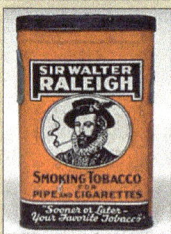

Raleigh commemorated on a tobacco can

1. Because of complicated politics beyond the scope of this chapter, Raleigh was not executed until fifteen years later, on October 29, 1618. On that day, Raleigh put on his best clothes and declared, "*I have a long journey to go, and therefore will I take my leave.*" After putting off his gown and doublet, he asked the executioner to show him the axe. "*This is a sharp medicine but it is a physician for all diseases.*"

While mounting the scaffold he also famously smoked a pipe of tobacco. This was to annoy King James, who detested tobacco and had even written a book called A COUNTERBLASTE TO TOBACCO alleging that the devil had brought it to England. (Actually, Raleigh gets credit for having popularized tobacco and making the Virginia Colony profitable.)

See RICH BEYER, THE GREATEST STORIES NEVER TOLD: 100 TALES FROM HISTORY TO ASTONISH, BEWILDER & STUPEFY 28 to 29 (2003) (noting that James I was an antismoking fanatic calling it "*a custom loathsome to the eye, hateful to the nose, harmful to the brain, dangerous to the lungs.*" In 1605, he increased tobacco taxes 4,000 percent to discourage its use.

About three centuries later, the Beatles in John Lennon's song "I'm So Tired" from *The White Album* also indicted Raleigh for tobacco: "*Although I'm so tired, I'll have another cigarette/And curse Sir Walter Raleigh, he was such a stupid get! [git].*" "Get" or "git" comes from Middle English and means an illegitimate offspring (bastard son of a bastard), related to "beget."

2. *Quoted in Crawford*, 541 U.S. at 45 (citations omitted).

3. *See Crawford*, 541 U.S. at 44 to 45 (citations omitted).

The BEATLES

The Beatles, better known as the *White Album* (1968) has no graphics or text other than the band's name and a serial number

4. "*In all criminal prosecutions, the accused shall enjoy the right to . . . be confronted with the witnesses against him . . . .*" U.S. CONST. amend. VI.

In addition, the Treason Clause protects these rights in the context of treason trials: "*No Person shall be convicted of Treason unless on the testimony of two Witnesses to the same overt Act, or on Confession in open court.*" U.S. CONST. art. III, § 3.

Just before the American Revolution, colonists such as Thomas Jefferson invoked Blackstone's third volume, identifying confrontation as incident to trial by jury. Graham at 218. Precursors to the Sixth Amendment were John Adams's Massachusetts and George Mason's Virginia constitutions. *Id.* at 216 to 17. Mason, over 150 years after Raleigh's execution, wrote the first American confrontation clause in 1776 in his room at Raleigh's Tavern in Williamsburg. *Id.* at 219.

Raleigh's Tavern in Williamsburg, Virginia

George Mason

Lilburne at every point outlined for the jury the unfairness of the process against him:

"*My prosecutors have had time enough to consult with counsel of all sorts and kinds to destroy me, yea, and with yourselves; and I have not had any time at all, not knowing in the least what you would charge upon me, and therefore could provide no defense for that which I knew not what it would be.*"[6]

But despite his repeated requests for a lawyer, Lilburne was on his own.[7]

In 1649, an accused had no right to representation. As one of his judges told him, *"counsel lies in matter of law, not of fact."* The idea here was that a defendant did not need a lawyer because no lawyer could present the facts better than the defendant himself. If a legal issue arose, the judge would be the defendant's counsel.[8]

Judge Keble: *Hear me one word, and you shall have two . . . your life is by law as dear as our lives, and our souls are at stake if we do you any wrong.*

Lilburne would have none of it:

"*If you will not allow me counsel. I have no more to say to you, you may murder me if you please.*"[9]

---

5. Our friend, John Lilburne, also argued for his confrontation rights in his Star Chamber trial of 1639, ten years before his 1649 trial featured in this chapter: "*produce them in the face of the open court, that we may see what they accuse me of; and I am ready here to answer for myself.*" Quoted in GRAHAM at 212 to 14 (arguing that Lilburne's experience had greater effect on the Puritan founders of America than Raleigh's trial).

6. Wolfram at 237. Lilburne's objects here to not getting the indictment before the trial in sufficient time to prepare a defense. Until the late nineteenth century in England, the defendant did not know the nature of the charge nor was he permitted to see the prosecution's depositions. J.M. Beattie, *Scales of Justice: Defense Counsel and the English Criminal Trial in the Eighteenth and Nineteenth Centuries*, 9 LAW & HIST. 221, 223 (1991). In America, the Sixth Amendment would guarantee defendants like Lilburne the right "*to be informed of the nature and cause of the accusation . . . .*" Coupled with the Fifth Amendment's guarantee of an indictment, Lilburne would have had no complaint. Even if Lilburne had gotten the indictment, he would probably not have been able to read it. Until 1362 indictments were written in French or Latin. During Cromwell's time indictments were in English but afterward went back to French or Latin. Not until 1751, under George II, were they written in English. See Wolfram at 229 n.58 (citing ORFIELD, CRIMINAL PROCEDURE FROM ARREST TO APPEAL 223 to 24 (1947)); see also POUND at 127.

7. Actually, not totally. Lilburne did have legal help present and spent a lot of time arguing that his solicitor, Mr. Sprat, be allowed to talk for him. See, e.g., Wolfram at 240. Lilburne succeeded in getting the court to allow him to have Mr. Sprat "*hold your papers and books.*" Id. Lilburne, however, could more than hold his own; not only could he argue better than judge and prosecutor, he was no slouch on trial objections:

> Attorney General: *What did lieutenant colonel Lilburne say to you concerning your pay? Did not he ask you . . .*
>
> Lilburne: *I pray, Sir, do not direct him what to say, but leave him to his own conscience and memory, and make him not for fear to swear more than his own conscience freely tells him is true.*

Many trial lawyers today miss this objection, which in its modern form is "*objection, leading.*" See Federal Rule of Evidence 611(c). Lawyers were excluded from most parts of the trial in 1539 and barred in all capital cases after 1670. KADRI at 58.

8. Lord Keble relied on the law at the time. **Lord Coke** had written that the accused only needed a lawyer if a legal issue presented: "*First, that the testimonies and the proofs of the offense ought to be so clear and manifest, as there can be no defense of it. Secondly, the court ought to be in stead of counsel for the prisoner, to see that nothing be urged against him contrary to law and right . . . .*" 3 COKE'S INSTITUTES fol. 29 (quoted in Wolfram at 236 n.81; also *The Third Part of the Institute of the Law of England: Concerning High Treason and Other Pleas of the Crown in Criminal Causes* at 29 (London M. Flesher, 1644)). In another context, Coke responded in 1613 to Jesuit jurists

that "*the law of England, is a law of mercy; . . . and it is far better for a prisoner to have a Judges [sic] opinion for him, than many counselors at the Bar; the Judges to have a special care . . . to see . . . that justice be done to the party.*" *King v. Thomas*, 80 Eng. Rep. 1022 (K.B. 1613), quoted in Westen at 86 n.59.

9. Wolfram at 236. Lilburne is playing to the jury. Also, he always had more to say.

John Lilburne faced a mode of trial far more streamlined than today; not having defense counsel made everything go faster. In fact there normally was no prosecutor either.[1] But as Lilburne's trial illustrates, judges often found it impossible to be the defendant's lawyer:

Judge Keble: *I hope the jury hath seen the evidence so plain and so fully that it doth confirm to them to do their dirty duty and find the prisoner guilty of what is charged upon him.*[2]

Judge Keble declared this before Lilburne had presented his defense, belying his prior statement to Lilburne that *"your life is by law as dear as our lives."*[3]

Even after hearing Lilburne's defense, Keble cheered for the prosecution:

Judge Keble: *. . . you will clearly find the like treason hatched in England.*[4]

Tudor-Stuart judges, as their Norman predecessors, held office at the pleasure of the crown.[5] The judge's job was to help the accuser, usually the victim, establish the prosecution case as well as be *"counsel for the defendant."*[6] The accused had to speak for himself and to respond to prosecution evidence when presented. If he did not defend himself, no one would do it for him.[7] The thinking of the time was that *"everyone of common understanding may as properly speak to a matter*

---

1. One thing to keep in mind is that the Lilburne, Raleigh, and Sir Thomas More trials were state trials with prosecutors. Generally, prosecutors were a rarity in criminal procedure. John H. Langbein, *The Origins of Public Prosecution at Common Law*, 17 Am. J. Legal Hist. 313, 315 (1973). For the average criminal case the judge-as-counsel system may have worked well enough. An average judge would have been just trying to get through his caseload. The jury decided the case after an inquest-type trial. Every juror knew the penalty for most felonies was death, and many probably knew or had heard of the defendant. Juries had a tradition of deciding the defendant's fate with the verdict of guilty or not guilty regardless of the evidence. In a relatively homogenous community this was rough justice. See generally Langbein, *Before the Lawyers*, at 288 to 89, 308, for examples of the procedures in normal cases.

2. *Quoted in* Wolfram at 247. Lilburne's trial followed the abuses of the Tudors and Stuarts, leading eventually to the end of the judge-as-counsel idea. Kiralfy at 364.

3. From the start, the judicial bias was clear. During the reading of the indictment Lilburne saw the prosecutor and judge whispering together:
Lilburne: *Hold a while, hold a while, let there be no discourse, but openly; for my adversaries or prosecutors whispering with the Judges, is contrary to the law of England, and extremely foul and dishonest play: and therefore I pray let me have no more of that injustice.*
Mr. Attorney: *It is nothing concerning you (let me give him satisfaction), it is nothing concerning you, Mr. Lilburne.*
Lilburne: *By your favor, Mr. Prideaux, that is more than I do know; but whether it be or not, by the express law of England, it ought not to be; therefore I pray let me have no more of it.*
This should have been the end of the issue, but Lilburne's judges seem to have been unable to avoid taking the bait and as the reading of the indictment droned on, one of the judges felt he had to justify himself:
Judge Thorp: *Mr. Lilburne, I desire to correct a mistake of yours in the law: You were pleased to condemn it as unjust, for the attorney-general's speaking with me when your indictment was a reading; you are to know, he is the prosecutor for the state here against you, and he must confer with us upon several occasions, and we with him, and this is law.*
Lilburne: *Not upon the bench, Sir, by your favour, unless it be openly, audibly, and avowedly, and not in any clandestine and whispering way: And by your favour, for all you are a judge, this is law, or else sir Edward Coke, in his 3d part instit. cap. high treason, or petty treason, hath published falsehoods, and the parliament hath licensed them; for their stamp in a special manner is to that book.*
Judge Thorp: *Sir Edward Coke is law, and he says, The attorney-general, or any other prosecutor may speak with us in open court, to inform us about the business before us in open court.*
Judge Thorp: *I tell you, Sir, the attorney-general may talk with any in the court, by law, as he did with me.*
Lilburne: *I tell you, Sir, it is unjust, and not warrantable by law, for him to talk with the court, or any of the judges thereof, in my absence, or in hugger-mugger, or by private whisperings.*

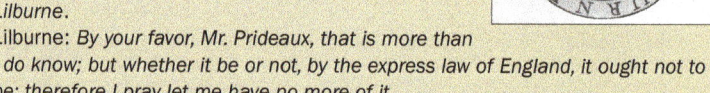

of fact as if he were the best lawyer . . . ."[8]

If a defense attorney was even there, his only role was to speak as to matters of law, leaving the defendant to fend for himself on any matter of fact.[9]

Certainly, most defendants were not up to the task, but Lilburne was:

"Truly, Sir, I am not daunted at the multitude of my judges, neither at the glittering of your scarlet robes, nor the majesty of your presence, and harsh austere deportment towards me, I bless my good God for it, who gives me courage and boldness."[10]

JUDGES START TO BECOME JUDGES

Lilburne's judges had a commission to get him executed. Since medieval times, judges were the king's law enforcers. Largely this remained their role through the Tudor monarchs, and Cromwell expected the same consideration once he was in charge.

Over time, though, judges had started to become trained professionals. Customarily they did their job with little oversight from the king. To the dismay of monarchs, judges started to become independent. An example of this happened a generation before Lilburne, with Sir Edward Coke, Lord Chief Justice of England.

Of Coke and King: Coke is a biggie in common-law history.[11]

Lord Keble: *No, Sir; it is no hugger-mugger for him to do as he did; spare your words, and burst not out into passion; for thereby you will declare yourself to be within the compass of your indictment, without any further proof . . .*
Even at this stage, Lilburne played to the jury, evident in his use of the common term "hugger-mugger." WEBSTER'S at 1211 ("*1. To act or confer stealthily. 2. To blunder along.*"). Lilburne makes his point despite, or perhaps using, the judges' protestations. His judges and prosecutor never bother to say what they were discussing, a point the jury could not have missed. Wolfram at 233 to 34.

4. Wolfram at 250.

5. *See* POUND at 134 (noting how American royal colonial governors, like their Stuart king masters, removed judges who did not decide as dictated). *See also* John H. Langbein, *The Historical Origins of the Privilege against Self-Incrimination at Common Law*, 92 MICH. L. REV. 1047, 1050 (1994) (discussing the limitations of court-as-counsel and citing Lilburne's trial judges as examples).

6. Talk about a conflict of interest! For example, John Hawles, in his 1689 tract, recognized that judges "*generally have betrayed their poor client, to please, as they apprehend their better client, the king.*" Langbein, *The Privilege*, at n.13.

7. J.M. BEATTIE, CRIME AND THE COURTS IN ENGLAND: 1660 to 1800, at 223 (1986).

8. William Hawkins, *A Treatise of the Pleas of the Crown* (London 1721). As John Langbein stated when discussing the history of the right to remain silent, "*the right to remain silent when no one can speak for you is simply the right to slit your throat, and it is hardly a mystery that the defendant did not hasten to avail themselves of such a privilege.*" Langbein, *The Privilege*, at 1054.

9. *See, e.g.*, BEATTIE at 360 (citing to a trial from the Surrey Assizes in 1752, where the judge explained "*your counsel knows his duty very well, they may indeed speak for you in any matter of law that may arise on your trial, but cannot as to matter of fact, for you must manage your defense in the best manner you can yourself.*" Cited in Langbein, *The Privilege*, at n.34).

10. Wolfram at 245. Lilburne made this statement in the closing argument for the jury's benefit.

11. Edward Coke. Coke was a prosecutor, law teacher, writer, a legal historian, and eventually the Lord Chief Justice of England. His INSTITUTES ON THE COMMON LAW OF ENGLAND is our main source for much of the history and procedure of the common law. Coke had been Speaker of the House in Parliament as well as Queen Elizabeth I's solicitor general at the same time. In this dual role he used any number of delaying tactics to defend royal prerogative. LEONARD W. LEVY, ORIGINS OF THE FIFTH AMENDMENT: THE RIGHT AGAINST SELF-INCRIMINATION 199 to 200 (1968).

Having dual roles in the executive and legislative branches did not bother seventeenth centaury potentates.

As for Coke's influence, Lilburne, a Puritan, would go to the House of Commons with a Bible in one hand and Coke's INSTITUTES in the other. Harold J. Berman, *Religious Foundations of Law in the West: An Historical Perspective*, 1 J.L. & RELIGION 3, 33 (1983).

Lilburne with either the Bible or Coke in hand

Three years after Coke secured Walter Raleigh's conviction, King James I had made Edward Coke (pronounced "Cook") chief justice of the Court of Common Pleas in 1606.

Once in this position, Coke led the judges of his day in asserting the supremacy of the common law over the other courts, both temporal and ecclesiastical. But even more than that, Coke fought for the supremacy of the rule of law over magnates, lords, and even the king.[1]

James I, however, was a big advocate of the divine right of kings—being one, it came easily to him.[2] In 1598 he wrote THE TRUE LAW OF FREE MONARCHIES, asserting among other things *rex est loquens* ("the king is the law speaking").[3]

Technically, James was not saying he was above the law but that he *was* the law—a debatable distinction.[4]

Coke did not buy the party line. In the Privy Council[5] in 1608, with the chief justices[6] and other potentates of the realm, Coke argued with Bishop Bancroft, who was acting as James's proxy. Relying on good old *Magna Carta* Chapter 29, Coke argued the king was not above the law.

Bancroft: *"All judges, temporal and ecclesiastical, are but delegates of the king who might repossess jurisdiction in whatever cases*

---

1. Coke's tool of choice in these jurisdictional disputes was the writ of habeas corpus: "*it manifestly appeareth, that no man ought to be imprisoned but for some certain cause ....*" Quoted in William F. Duker, English Origins of the Writ of Habeas Corpus: A Peculiar Path to Fame, 53 N.Y.U. L. REV. 983, 984 (1978).

2. Among other arrogations, James thought himself the end all of criminal procedure. On his coronation trip from Edinburgh to London he had an alleged pickpocket hanged without trial. *Reported in* LEVY at 206. The reaction of Sir John Harrington sums up the what Englishmen thought: "*I hear our new king has hanged one man before he was tried; it is strangely done: now if the wind bloweth thus, why may not a man be tried before he has offended?*" *Id.* at 473 n.1.

James I of England (and James VI of Scotland)

3. *See* LEVY at 243. During the reign of James's son, Charles I, in 1644 Samuel Rutherford would write *Lex, Rex* ("*The Law is King*"), expounding the theological arguments for the rule of law over the rule of men and kings. *See* The Liberty Library of Constitutional Classics, http://www.constitution.org/sr/lexrex.htm (last visited December 5, 2005).

4. Lest you think this concept is dead, look to President Richard Nixon's statement during his 1977 interviews with David Frost: "*When the President does it, that means it is not illegal.*" *See* Frost/Nixon (Universal Studios 2008) (dramatizing the Frost-Nixon interviews of 1977).

5. Privy Council. In England this started out as the king's council of close advisors, thus the name "privy," for private. Later, powerful sovereigns would use the Privy Council to circumvent the courts and Parliament. For example, a committee of the council, which later became the Court of the Star Chamber, could inflict any punishment except death without regard to evidence rules or the burden of proof. Henry VIII, "*on the advice of the Council,*" enacted laws by mere proclamation, and Parliament did not regain prominence until after Henry VIII's death. In 1553 the council had forty members, making it ineffective as an advisory body. Smaller committees developed that evolved into the modern cabinet. *Privy Council* 9 THE NEW ENCYCLOPEDIA BRITANNICA 713 (15th ed. 2002).

6. How Many Chief Justices Do You Need? At this point in history there was more than one "Chief Justice" in England. The three high common-law courts—the Court of Common Pleas, the Court of the King's (or Queen's) Bench, and the Court of the Exchequer—each had its own chief justice. That of the Exchequer Court was styled as the lord chief baron of the Exchequer, and that of the Common Pleas was Chief Justice of the Court of Common Pleas, leaving the head of the King's (or Queen's) Bench to be known simply as the Lord Chief Justice. The courts were combined in 1875, leaving a single Chief Justice. In this, the law went

Bishop Bancroft

he pleased. This was clear in divinity that such authority belongs to the king . . ."

Coke: "But under Magna Carta Chapter 39, the king cannot personally decide any case nor remove any from his courts of justice; the judges alone decide this.⁷"

King James: "*Common law judges are like papists who quote scripture and then put forth their interpretation to be unquestioned!*⁸ *I, the king, am the Supreme Judge and all courts are under me. If I choose, I may sit on the bench and decide cases.*⁹ *The law is founded on reason, which I possess, and I, the king, protect the law.*"

Coke: "*The king lacks legal knowledge and the law protects both the king and the subjects.*"

Now James was really angry. Rising, he shook his fist in Coke's face. Although Coke had used diplomatic phraseology in saying that the "*law protects the king*" rather than the king is under the law, James saw right through it.

"*Yours is traitorous speech! The king protects the law, not the law the king!*"

Coke, no dummy, fell on all fours begging the king's pardon, which James eventually gave.¹⁰

So ended the incident, for the time being.¹¹

---

full circle. Before King Edward I's reign all these functions were under the office of *justiciar*, roughly equivalent to the modern prime minister.

7. Levy at 243 (stating that Coke cited *Magna Carta* Chapter 39, but depending on the numbering system, this is also numbered Chapter 29):
  "*No free man shall be taken or imprisoned or disseised or outlawed or exiled or in any way ruined, nor will we go or send against him, except by the lawful judgment of his peers or by the law of the land.*"

8. Being called a "papist" was not a good thing in post-Reformation England. Given the weakness of *Magna Carta* as precedent, James's statement may not have been so wrong. Yet in these arguments all the Stuarts (with the possible exception of James's grandson Charles II) seem to miss the big picture: the era of "divine right" legitimating power was passing.

9. Actually, James was historically correct. *See* Baker Legal History, at 98. The Norman kings did just this. Also, Coke's argument that *Magna Carta* limited the king's power on this point is unconvincing. In fact *Magna Carta* Chapter 18 requires the king to be more active in justice administration. What the barons extracted from a weak King John in 1215 was not a limitation on the king's power to hear a case but the exact opposite: a demand that the king, or the king's proxies (i.e., his judges), come more often to hear cases. *See* Danziger & Gillingham at 177 ("*As a rule Magna Carta set limits to what the king could do; but in this one clause he was required to give more, rather than less, government.*").

King James I

10. What we have of the meeting comes from various sources including Coke's own account. In these sources, especially Coke's, it is hard to tell what is a verbatim transcription and what he added later.
  See generally Catherine Drinker Bowen, The Lion and the Throne: The Life and Times of Sir Edward Coke 302 to 06 (1956);Levy at 243 to 44. This Coke history was well known during colonial times in both America and Britain. *Id.* at 243.

11. This was a petty way for James to win the argument. James might have well just said, "*It's good to be the king!*" *See* History of the World, Part I (20th Century Fox 1981).

Coke the Unrepentant: Begging and receiving King James's pardon did not change Coke. He kept on with his *Magna Carta* Chapter 29 arguments and issuing writs of prohibition against the ecclesiastical courts' use of the *ex officio oath*.[1]

At this point, the common-law courts defined ecclesiastical court jurisdiction. This was the result of the long struggle between the king's common-law courts and the Catholic Church's ecclesiastical courts. The irony here is that kings from Henry II and after pushed for the supremacy of the various king's courts as they fought for control with Rome. Now, the "king's" common-law courts were limiting what were now the king's ecclesiastical courts. No wonder James was miffed! James was to remark on the chief justice's *"perverseness"* and that *"[m]y spirit shall be no longer be vexed with this man."*[2]

So what was James to do? Coke had become popular with the people and the House of Commons. Besides, James had nothing for which he could punish Coke.

James decided to promote Coke out of his problematical position of Chief Justice of Common Pleas and make him Chief Justice of the King's Bench, that is, Chief Justice of England. James also made Coke a member of the Privy Council to seduce him even more.[3] It did not work. Coke continued standing up for the ideal of the common law, and, in 1616, James finally dismissed him.[4]

Judges were becoming judges, not just the king's men or law enforcement. They were beginning to view themselves under the law, not just under the king, and the king was under the law as well. And the main tool these judges used to advance the rule of law was the writ of habeas corpus.

THE WRIT OF HABEAS CORPUS

"The privilege of the Writ of Habeas Corpus shall not be suspended, unless when in Cases of Rebellion or Invasion, the public Safety may require it."

—U.S Const. art. I, § 9

---

1. A *Writ of Prohibition* is an order from a superior court limiting an inferior court's actions, often defining jurisdiction. The counterpart is the *Writ of Mandamus*, ordering an inferior court to do something.

If you are interested in an extensive academic debate (or just have insomnia) on the use of the Writ of Prohibition and its role in the development of the privilege against self-incrimination, see Charles M. Gray, *Prohibitions and the Privilege against Self-Incrimination,* in Tudor Rule and Revolution: Essays for G.R. Elton from His American Friends 345 (Delloyd J. Guth & John W. McKenna eds., 1982).

2. Levy at 249. Unlike with King Henry II back in 1170, and his comment that led to the murder of Thomas Becket, discussed in Chapter 1, James's statement did not appear to have inspired anyone to snuff out the Chief Justice.

James I

3. Levy at 252 to 54. James got the idea from Frances Bacon, his solicitor general, who defended royal prerogative by arguing that the common law was just the crown's servant and the twelve common-law judges were the twelve lions supporting Solomon's throne. *Id.* at 254. (This argument had to have appealed to James's vanity and shows Bacon to be a toady of the first order.) Though Coke was busy advancing the common law and Bacon was busy becoming the first real scientist in modern history, they found time to detest each other.

4. Levy 254.
Coke outlived James by nine years. Consequently, James never got around to getting back at Coke. James's son, Charles, did. In 1634 Charles's lackeys searched Coke's house while Coke was on his deathbed for *"seditious and dangerous papers."* They stole everything they could get their hands on, nearly all his writings, including manuscripts of his legal works, jewelry, money, and valuables. They even took his will. It took his heirs seven years to get any of it back, and they never got the will. See Nelson B. Lasson, The History and Development of the Fourth Amendment to the United States Constitution 31 to 32 (1937); Samuel Dash, The Intruders: Unreasonable Searches and Seizures from King John to John Ashcroft 21 to 22 (2004).

We know habeas corpus today as "the great writ" for its role in securing individual liberty.[5] But habeas corpus did not start as a tool to guard individual liberty.[6]

Originally, the king's traveling judges used it to get jurisdiction over a defendant who was otherwise not present. It was a way of securing a party's appearance after other more lenient ways did not work.[7] Thus it functioned more like a modern summons, arrest warrant, or extradition order, or for a person in custody.[8]

Later judges of one court would use the writ of habeas corpus to get jurisdiction over individuals and their cases (*"causa"*) from other courts. This is a function like the modern use of the writ to secure the rights of individuals or their causes, known then as the *habeas corpus cum causa*.

The "king's judges" would use habeas corpus against the ecclesiastical court to limit their jurisdiction in favor of "the king's" (i.e., common-law) courts. This is what the kings wanted when the church courts belonged to Rome. But since Henry VIII, the ecclesiastical courts were the king's ecclesiastical courts.[9]

The king's judges, like Edward Coke, turned the writ of habeas corpus back on the king by using it to limit the jurisdiction of the ecclesiastical courts.[10] This challenged the very notion that justice flowed from the king to the subjects.

Courts, through habeas corpus, were emancipating themselves from the king's rule to follow the rule of law. The proponents of this view created a history that the writ of habeas corpus sprang somehow from *Magna Carta* as a basic right.[11]

As we have seen, Oliver Cromwell was no more a supporter of judicial independence than the Stuarts. But the Habeas Corpus Act of 1679 came from this period and is the precursor to the habeas corpus rights in the American Constitution.[12]

This is the role of the writ of habeas corpus today: to limit the executive branch's prerogatives, whether kings or American presidents.[13]

---

5. A writ is just lawyer-speak for "order."

6. Habeas corpus. Latin for "you have the body," commands a person detaining another to produce the prisoner. The issue is the legality of the detention, not guilt or innocence. Habeas corpus is *"the great writ of liberty"* issuing from the common-law courts of Chancery, King's Bench, Common Pleas, and Exchequer. BLACK'S at 638 to 39. See U.S. CONST. art. I, § 9.

7. See Duker at 1000.

Coke

8. This is still the purpose of the modern *writ of habeas corpus ad prosecundum*. The original habeas corpus writ was the *habeas corpus ad respondendum*, directing a sheriff or other official to produce the body (the *"corpus"*) of a party to respond (*"ad respondendum"*) in court. Duker at 992, 996 and 1007.

9. Duker at 1018 to 23.

10. Duker at 1031 to 36.

11. Duker at 1031.

12. The U.S. CONSTITUTION, Article I, Section 9, states that *"[t]he privilege of the Writ of Habeas Corpus shall not be suspended, unless when in Cases of Rebellion or Invasion, the public Safety may require it.* For a copy of Habeas Corpus Act of 1679....", see http://press-pubs.uchicago.edu/founders/documents/a1_9_2s2.html (last visited Feb. 26, 2008).

13. See, e.g., *Hamdi v. Rumsfeld*, 542 U.S. 507 (2004) (holding that Yaser Esam Hamdi, a U.S. citizen being detained indefinitely as an "illegal enemy combatant" must have the ability to challenge this detention before an impartial judge). For a good, brief outline of the history of habeas corpus and its modern application, see James Robertson, *Quo Vadis, Habeas Corpus?* 55 BUFF. L. REV. 1063 (2008).

JUDICIAL INDEPENDENCE

One of the great grievances against the Stuarts was their lack of respect for judicial independence.[1] In 1688, the Glorious Revolution removed the final Stuart king, James II. Parliament gave the realm to William III and Mary but only under the condition that they recognize various civil rights, which eventually culminated in the Act of Settlement of 1701, the Act of Succession, and the English Bill of Rights.

Among many rights, it provided that only both houses of Parliament in agreement could remove a judge.[2] Moreover, judges would keep their job *quamdiu se bene gesserint* ("during good behavior").

Judges at last were free to follow the law, not just the whim of a monarch, as William Blackstone noted some decades later:

"[T]he court must pronounce that judgment [sentence] which the law has annexed to the crime, and which has been constantly mentioned, together with the crime itself, in some or other of the former chapters."[3]

When judges were the king's men, they had considerable discretionary power to exercise "the king's" prerogative pardon powers.[4] Now, despite the fact that English courts are still "the King's (or Queen's) Bench,"[5] Parliament appoints the judges and is the only entity that can remove a judge for cause.[6]

Any modern court views the "rule of law" as ultimate

---

1. *See* Fisher at 617 to 18 and n. 163.

2. **Act of Settlement** (12 & 13 Will., 3 c.2 (Eng.)) also settled succession to the English throne on the Electress Sophia of Hanover, a granddaughter of James I, and her Protestant heirs. It remains the main Act of Parliament governing succession to the throne.

3. 4 BLACKSTONE, COMMENTARIES ON THE LAWS OF ENGLAND 369 to 72 (1st ed. 1769).

4. On judges gaining the king's discretionary power over pardons, see Thomas A. Green, *The Jury and the English Law of Homicide, 1200 to 1600*, 74 MICH L. REV. 414, 425 (1976). During the Middle Ages this had much to do with practicality. A convict was hanged within hours of conviction. Thus, for the king's pardoning power to work, the king's representative (the judge) in conjunction with the jury had to decide without delay whether the defendant deserved pardon.

5. The **Queen's Bench** (or **King's Bench**, for a male monarch) is now a division of the High Court of Justice of England and Wales. Subdivisions include the Commercial Court, the Admiralty Court, and the Administrative Court. It is also the name of the superior court in the Canadian provinces of Saskatchewan, Alberta, New Brunswick, and Manitoba. The *Law Reports* use the abbreviation QB (or KB) in legal citations.

6. The Act of Settlement of 1701 gave judicial appointments to Parliament. This had the effect of subordinating the common law to statute law. LOVELL at 412. As discussed above, the Framers did not intend this subordination for America. *See Marbury v. Madision*, 5 U.S. (1 Cranch) 137 (1803).

James II

Blackstone

authority. Certainly, law comes from Parliament or Congress, but judges must be free to apply the law. This idea goes far back to Aristotle and his requirement that judges apply the law

"to redress the inequality which is this kind of justice identified with injustice."[7]

To Aristotle, an equitable or just decision is what the legislator would have decided in the particular circumstances if he had been present. For this reason judges and juries had to have separate powers from legislators.[8]

As discussed, judges in England started out as law enforcement and as the "king's judges," to affect his rule and laws, or the "king's peace." Parliament took them over and became supreme over the king and his courts.

America was different.

The Framers of the American Constitution specifically rejected the notion of parliamentary supremacy as the exclusive basis of government.

The Declaration of Independence's indictment of King George III, for instance, was a legal fiction; it was really an indictment of Parliament's actions, such as the Stamp Act, the Intolerable Acts, etc.

Thus, for America, the Framers created a government with separation of powers where judges are supposed to have power and independence to apply the law and Constitution.[9]

This was how the Framers ensured the rule of law.

7. The following is **Aristotle** in context: "*The law never looks beyond the question, what damage was done? And it treats the parties involved as equals. All it asks is whether an injustice has been done or an injury by one party on the other. Consequently, what the judge seeks to do is to redress the inequality, which is this kind of justice identified with injustice. Thus in a case of assault or homicide the action and the consequences of the action may be represented as a line divided into equal parts ... What the judge aims at doing is to make the parts equal by the penalty he imposes ..."* ARISTOTLE, ETHICS 148 to 49 (Penguin Classics ed. 1955).

8. Lawmakers pass general laws prospectively, "*while ... the juror [is] actually judging present and specific cases.*" ARISTOTLE, RHETORIC 32 (George A. Kennedy trans., 2d ed. 2007), quoted in Robert Stein, Rule of Law: What Does It Mean? 18 MINN. J. INT'L L. 293, 297 (2009).

9. See *The Ninth & Tenth Amendments*, in this series, published by **Constitution Press, 2017** regarding judicial discretion. For the cautionary tale of what happens when judicial independence is lost, see JUDGMENT AT NUREMBERG (United Artists 1961), a fictionalized film account of the Nuremberg Trials after WWII. Stanley Kramer directed Spencer Tracy as the American judge trying to understand how German judges could have condoned Nazi crimes against humanity.

THE FRAMERS AND THE RULE OF LAW

The Framers believed in the rule of law.[1] Indeed, the entire premise of the American Revolution was to "re-establish" the rule of law from a despotic king.[2]

Or as Thomas Paine forcefully extolled in COMMON SENSE in 1776,

"the world may know, that so far as we approve of monarchy, that in America THE LAW IS KING. *For as in absolute governments the King is law, so in free countries the law* OUGHT *to be King; and there ought to be no other."*

The Declaration of Independence, in addition to declaring *"inalienable rights,"* indicted King

---

1. The world "legal" has Indo-European roots and comes to English from Latin, as Thomas Aquinas wrote:

"Law is a rule and measure of acts whereby man is induced to act or is restrained from acting: For lex (law) is derived from ligare (to bind), because it binds one to act."

Thus, the Latin *"ligare"* is also in the English *"ligature"* because what is "legal" is what binds. It is also the root of the Latin *"legere"* ("to read") as in to "bind with the written word." Modern Spanish has *"leer"* ("to read"), which is seen in the English verb "leer," as in to stare at someone.

The Roman/Latin for "law"(*"ius"*) had two meanings: objective rules of actions and subjective rights to act. Thus, although the Romans had a limited concept of individual rights, they did have the framework of rule of law. SUSAN FORD WILTSHIRE, GREECE, ROME AND THE BILL OF RIGHTS 86 (1992).

2. Jacob Reynolds, *The Rule of Law and the Origins of the Bill of Attainder Clause*, 18 ST. THOMAS L. REV. 177, 187 (2006).

The concept of the rule of law connected to democracy is old in European tradition. Iceland boasts the oldest democratic assembly with the lawspeaker, the "skapti thoroddsson", speaking from the "law rock", "the althing". KADRI at 22.

The "**Alþingi**," Anglicized variously as "althing" or "althingi" (literally the "all-thing"), is still Iceland's national parliament, founded in 930 AD.

The word "parliament" comes from the French "*parler,*" KYNELL at 108, still evident in the English word "parlor" and "parley."

An Icelandic stamp with the LOGSOGUMATHAR ALTHING ("lawspeaker at the althing").

3. THE DECLARATION OF INDEPENDENCE shows the import of the rule of law. After the Preamble, the Declaration indicts King George III for not following the rule of law:

"He has refused his Assent to Laws, the most wholesome and necessary for the public good.

He has forbidden his Governors to pass Laws of immediate and pressing importance, unless suspended in their operation till his Assent should be obtained; and when so suspended, he has utterly neglected to attend to them.

He has refused to pass other Laws for the accommodation of large districts of people, unless those people would relinquish the right of Representation in the Legislature, a right inestimable to them and formidable to tyrants only.

He has called together legislative bodies at places unusual, uncomfortable, and distant from the depository of their Public Records, for the sole purpose of fatiguing them into compliance with his measures.

He has dissolved Representative Houses repeatedly, for opposing with manly firmness of his invasions on the rights of the people.

He has refused for a long time, after such dissolutions, to cause others to be elected, whereby the Legislative Powers, incapable of Annihilation, have returned to the People at large for their exercise; the State remaining in the mean time

George III for failing to uphold the law.[3]

The Framers read Aristotle:

"*It is more proper that the law should govern than any of the citizens [and] persons holding supreme power should be appointed only guardians and servants of the law.*"[4]

They read the Enlightenment thinkers, including John Locke:

"*Freedom of men under government is to have a standing rule to live by, common to every one of that society, and made by the legislative power erected in it; a liberty to follow my own will in all things, where that rule prescribes not: and not to be subject to the inconstant, uncertain, arbitrary will of another man.*"[5]

---

exposed to all the dangers of invasion from without, and convulsions within.

He has endeavoured to prevent the population of these States; for that purpose obstructing the Laws for Naturalization of Foreigners; refusing to pass others to encourage their migrations hither, and raising the conditions of new Appropriations of Lands.

He has obstructed the Administration of Justice by refusing his Assent to Laws for establishing Judiciary Powers. He has made Judges dependent on his Will alone for the tenure of their offices, and the amount and payment of their salaries."

4. *Quoted in* Reynolds *at* 185 *and* n.45. "Anyone," Aristotle wrote, "who bids the law to rule seems to bid god and intellect alone to rule, but anyone who bids a human being to rule adds on also the wild beast." ARISTOTLE, POLITICS bk. III, ch. 16, at 111 (Peter L.P. Simpson trans., Univ. of North Carolina Press 1997), *quoted in* Stein *at* 297. For Aristotle, the rule of law trumps majority rule.

Locke

Rutherford

Montesquieu

Grotius

5. Locke, quoted in Reynolds at 179.

In addition to Locke, the Founders read Samuel Rutherford's *Lex, Rex* ("*The Law is King*") (1644), giving the theoretical foundation of the rule of law. Rutherford in turn influenced Charles Montesquieu's THE SPIRIT OF THE LAWS (1748). From there came the U.S. Constitution, which provided the subject of Alexis de Tocqueville's study, DEMOCRACY IN AMERICA.

de Tocqueville

God thinking about what Grotius wrote

For the Enlightenment even God is subject to the rule of law. Hugo Grotius's LAWS OF WAR AND PEACE I, i, x (1625), the origin of all international law, states that: "*Measureless as is the power of God, nevertheless it can be said that there are certain things over which that power does not extend …. Just as even God cannot cause that two times two should not make four, so He cannot cause that which is intrinsically evil be not evil.*" Quoted in WILTSHIRE at 68.

"*Even the will of an omnipotent being cannot change or abrogate*" natural law, which "*would maintain its objective validity even if we should assume the impossible, that there is no God or that he does not care for human affairs.*"

Much later, Sigmund Freud would offer another explanation of the source of the rule of law:

"*Civilization obtains mastery over the individual's dangerous desire for aggression by weakening and disarming it and by setting up an agency within him to watch over it, like a garrison in a conquered city.*"

Freud, *quoted in* KADRI *at* 14. One of the things garrisoning that aggression is the rule of law.

Freud

And they went to the movies!

Well, not really; they went to the theater to see Joseph Addison's play *Cato, A Tragedy* (1712) about the ancient Roman Cato fighting to save the Roman Republic from Julius Caesar.[1] The play underscored the Founders' fear of those who would subvert the republic and the rule of law.

Cato lost.[2] But the play may have given us some of the American Revolution's best lines:

Patrick Henry, for instance, may have got

"Give me Liberty or give me death!"[3]

from *Cato* Act II, Scene 4:

"It is not now time to talk of aught/But chains or conquest, liberty or death."

Also, Nathan Hale's valediction,

"I regret that I have but one life to lose for my country"[4]

may have come from Act IV, Scene 4:

"What a pity it is/That we can die but once to serve our country."

---

1. RICHARD BROOKHISER, WHAT WOULD THE FOUNDERS DO?: OUR QUESTIONS, THEIR ANSWERS 24 to 25 (2006). Washington had the play performed for his men at Valley Forge during the winter of 1777 to 78.

John Kemblein playing the Roman Cato in Addison's play

Cato the Younger

2. *Cato the Younger* (95–46 BC), was a politician and statesman in the late Roman Republic, remembered for his lengthy conflict against Julius Caesar and his moral integrity. When Caesar finally defeated him, Cato refused to surrender and took his own life. WILTSHIRE at 29.

3. Henry, though, may never have said, *"Give me liberty orgive me death!"* The speech did not appear in print until William Wirt's LIFE AND CHARACTER OF PATRICK HENRY (1817), and historians speculate that Wirt invented it after the fact.

Patrick Henry before the House of Burgesses by Peter F. Rothermel (1851)

4. Nathan Hale (1755–1776) was a Continental Army soldier during the American Revolution and America's first spy. The British captured and hanged him. Although he was only twenty-one when he died, he made it on a postage stamp in 1925 and 1929.

5. "Loyalty," echoed Justice Hugo Black in 1960, *"comes from love of good government, not fear of a bad one."* BLACK'S at 881.

6. How about STAR WARS (20th Century Fox 1977), with the virtuous Jedi knights fighting the evil empire to bring back the old republic? The empire's admirals, generals, and evil emperor Palpatine even have British accents!

For the Framers a republic was the best government and the way to achieve true civic virtue.[5] They, like Cato, were set to fight against an empire: the British Empire. A virtuous republic fighting against an evil empire is an American archetype.[6]

The Framers put it all together to make a democratic republic *"to the end that it may be a government of laws and not of men"* as John Adams provided in the Massachusetts Constitution of 1780.[7] James Madison's FEDERALIST No. 51 noted:

"If men were angels, no government would be necessary. If angels were to govern men, neither external nor internal controls on government would be necessary. In framing a government which is to be administered by men over men, the great difficulty lies in this: you must first enable the government to control the governed; and in the next place oblige it to control itself."[8]

With the possible exception to Madison's reference to angels, Adams, Madison, Locke, and Aristotle could have written each other's sentences.

Ronald Reagan at Berlin's Brandenburg Gate, challenging Gorbachev to *"Tear down this wall!"* on June 12, 1987

And don't forget Ronald Regan decrying the Soviet Union as an *"evil empire"* to the National Association of Evangelicals in Orlando, Florida, on March 8, 1983.

Reagan giving the *"evil empire"* speech

7. John Adams's Massachusetts constitution stands as the famous exposition of separation of powers as the basis for the rule of law:
"*In the government of this commonwealth, the legislative department shall never exercise the executive and judicial powers or either of them: the executive shall never exercise the legislative and judicial powers, or either of them: the judicial shall never exercise the legislative and executive powers, or either of them:* **to the end it may be a government of laws and not of men.**"
MASSACHUSETTS CONSTITUTION, Part the First, art. XXX (1780) (emphasis added).

8. For a discussion of antecedents to the American rule of law tradition, see Steven G. Calabresi, *The Historical Origins of the Rule of Law in the American Constitutional Order*, 28 HARV. J.L. & PUB. POL'Y 273 (2005). Regarding law in the early colonies, see, for example, William E. Nelson, *Authority and the Rule of Law in Early Virginia*, 29 OHIO N.U. L. REV. 305 (2003); William E. Nelson, *The Utopian Legal Order of the Massachusetts Bay Colony, 1630 to 1686*, 47 AM. J. LEGAL HIST. 183 (2005).

Thus the Framers not only knew the value of the rule of law but also the difficulty in structuring a democratic republic to give it effect. As Aristotle warned,

"now, anyone who bids the law to rule seems to bid god and intellect alone to rule, but anyone who bids a human being to rule adds on also the wild beast. For desire is such a beast, and spiritedness perverts rulers even when they are the best of men. Hence law is intellect without appetite."[1]

Roger Sherman followed in 1787 when he wrote that *"[n]o bill of rights ever yet bound the supreme power longer than the honeymoon of a new married couple, unless the rulers were interested in preserving the rights."*[2]

With this problem in mind, the Framers sought a way to structure their new republic so it would last.

To make it last, they divided the power among three branches of government with a system of checks and balances.[3] This gave the rulers, exercising political power in conjunction with and in opposition to the other branches of government, an interest in preserving individual rights.

The power of judicial review is part of this system to assure individual rights, such as the right to a lawyer.

THE DEFENDANT GETS LILBURNE'S LAWYER

Again back to Lilburne pleading for counsel:

"I am sure by common equity and justice that I may have counsel and solicitors also assigned me."[4]

---

1. THE POLITICS OF ARISTOTLE (350 B.C.), quoted in Scott D. Gerber, *The Court, the Constitution, and the History of Ideas*, 61 VAND. L. REV. 1067 (2008).

2. Roger Sherman, writing in the New Haven Gazette quoted in Seymour W. Warfel, *Quartering of Troops: The Unlitigated Third Amendment*, 21 TENN. L. REV. 723, 727 (1951).

Roger Sherman (1721 to 93) served on the Committee of Five that drafted the DECLARATION OF INDEPENDENCE and became a representative and senator. He was the only person to sign the four great American state papers: THE CONTINENTAL ASSOCIATION, the DECLARATION OF INDEPENDENCE, the ARTICLES OF CONFEDERATION, and the CONSTITUTION.

Civil War general William Tecumseh Sherman was a distant descendant, and Watergate-era prosecutor Archibald Cox was a direct descendant of Sherman.

Roger Sherman

William Tecumseh Sherman

Archibald Cox

3. Because British merchants had the largest amount of liquid capital, there was little reason not to have them present at Parliament for money matters. Because they were commoners, it made sense that all bills relating to money or taxation start in the House of Commons. Following this, the U.S. CONSTITUTION provides that all money bills begin in the House of Representatives. U.S. CONST. art. I, § 7. LOVELL at 185 n.11, 196.

4. Wolfram at 236.

5. Cromwell proved himself no more principled than the Stuarts in this use of "trials" for utilitarian ends. Cromwell, as the monarchs before him, used the law of "high treason," which had its roots in the ancient Germanic relationship of faith between a lord and his men. This is why even in modern times the murder of a husband by the wife, or the master by the servant, was not just murder but "petit treason."

Lilburne's trial followed a long line of state cases where the crown had used the legal form of the trial to affect the ruler's wishes.[5] Generally, that meant killing somebody for high treason.

By no means was Lilburne's trial of 1649 the end of it. Less than twenty years later the Popish Plot trials occurred.

The Popish Plot: The Popish Plot (1678–81) was a conspiracy to discredit English Catholics hatched by two corrupt English clergymen, Titus Oates and Israel Tonge. They fabricated that a "popish plot" existed to murder King Charles II and replace him with his Roman Catholic brother James. Charles II did not believe Oates, but the conspiracy took a life of its own, fueled by anti-Catholicism.[6] King Charles, who already had problems appearing too Catholic because he had a Catholic wife, could stop neither Oates nor the hysteria.[7]

Oates initially made forty-three allegations against various members of Catholic religious orders, including Jesuits and numerous Catholic nobles.[8] At one point Charles personally interrogated Oates, catching him in a number of lies, and ordered his arrest. But Parliament later forced Oates's release.

The trials before Lord Chief Justice Sir William Scroggs were notorious because the defendants did not have lawyers and could not testify on their own behalf.[9] Oates had his victims at a disadvantage. He testified against them under oath, whereas they could only defend with their own unsworn statements.

---

6. Oates was a bad person. He had been an Anglican priest but the church dismissed him from various posts for "*drunken blasphemy,*" theft, and allegations of sodomy. In 1677 he became a chaplain aboard HMS *Adventurer* but was soon accused of buggery (a capital offense) and spared only because he was clergy. Oates fled England and joined the Catholic Order of the Jesuits, later claiming it was just to learn their secrets. When he returned to London he befriended the rabid anti-Catholic clergyman Israel Tonge and the two hatched the alleged "plot." Oates's Plot, THE CATHOLIC ENCYCLOPEDIA, http://www.newadvent.org/cathen/11173c.htm (last visited July 11, 2007).

7. As part of the hysteria, Parliament passed a bill excluding all Catholics from Parliament. In the streets people played with Popish Plot playing cards lauding Oates, including "*Oates uncovers the plot*" and "*The executions of the 5 Jesuits.*"

Set of common tiles at the time illustrating the so called "Popish Plot."

8. Sixteen innocent men were executed in direct connection with the plot, and eight others executed for being Catholic priests in the persecution that followed. The names of the executed are: in 1678 Edward Coleman (December 3); in 1679, John Grove, William Ireland, S.J. (January 24) Robert Green, Lawrence Hill (February 21), Henry Berry (February 28), Thomas Pickering, O.S.B. (May 14), Richard Langhorn (June 14), John Gavan, S.J., William Harcourt, S.J., Anthony Turner, S.J., Thomas Whitebread, S.J., John Fenwick, S.J. (June 20); in 1680, Thomas Thwing (October 23), William Howard, Viscount Stafford (December 29); and in 1681, Oliver Plunkett, Archbishop of Armagh (July 1). Those executed as priests were in 1679, William Plessington (July 19), Philip Evans, John Lloyd (July 22), Nicholas Postgate (August 7), Charles Mahony (August 12), John Wall (aka, Francis Johnson), O.S.F., John Kemble (August 22), and Charles Baker (aka David Lewis), S.J. (August 27). Oates's Plot, The CATHOLIC ENCYCLOPEDIA, http://www.newadvent.org/cathen/11173c.htm (last visited July 11, 2007).

9. As Fisher at 618 to 23 argues, the oath was still the basis of the criminal justice system's legitimacy, which could not tolerate conflicting oaths.

Oates got a state apartment and a £1,200 allowance from Parliament. Purges of Catholics spread, as did rumors of plots and French Catholic invasions. At least fifteen innocent "popish plotters" died the horrible traitor's death.[1]

As King Charles moved against him, Oates grew even bolder. He eventually denounced the king, which was strange because the supposed original plot was to kill Charles.

Oates eventually was punished but only for a while. Charles arrested and tried Oates for sedition and sentenced him to prison and a fine of £100,000.[2] When James II became king, he had Oates retried and sentenced to pillory, public whippings, and prison—and had him defrocked.[3] Ironically, some of the same Jesuits who had been at the mercy of Oates's sworn testimony could now testify against him and Oates, as a defendant, could not.

But the injustices of the law as applied, including Lilburne's trial and Oates's Popish Plot, lead to reform. This reform was the foundation of our Sixth Amendment.

THE TREASON ACT OF 1696

Just over ten years after the Popish Plot, Parliament passed the Treason Act of 1696.[4] One of the main reforms was guaranteeing the accused the right to counsel in treason cases—about fifty years too late for Lilburne but his legacy nonetheless.[5]

But this created a strange anomaly in the law: an accused had the right to a lawyer in a treason case, and in a misdemeanor case, but not with a felony charge.[6] Thus a person could still face the death penalty without the right to any legal help.

Much of this had to do with social class. Treason defendants tended to be powerful people or, at least, powerful at one time. They could afford a lawyer.[7] But in addition to social class, there were other reasons unique to treason trials that argued for a lawyer for the defendant.

---

1. For example, Edward Coleman, sentenced to death on December 3, 1678, was hanged, drawn, and quartered.

Coleman drawn to his execution.

2. Judge George Jeffreys declared that Oates was a *"Shame to mankind."* Following James II, King William of Orange and Queen Mary pardoned Oates in 1688, and Parliament gave him a pension. Oates died in 1705.

Judge Jeffries himself was no gem. He was *"the most consummate bully ever known in his profession"* and took *"a delight in misery merely as misery."* See LORD MACAULAY, THE HISTORY OF ENGLAND 73 to 75 (1979) (describing Judge Jeffreys).

Judge George Jeffreys

3. Oates's punishment became a precursor to the Eighth Amendment because at the time it was "unusual" for a common law court to defrock a clergyman.

For one thing, the Tudors, Stuarts, and Cromwell did not pick treason trial judges for their impartiality. Defendants like Sir Thomas More and John Lilburne knew this all too well. Treason law was complex. The government always managed to have its lawyer there to prosecute.[8] Thus treason trials were different in character from the short, simple trial of the average guy.

The Treason Act, at least, recognized that a lawyer makes one's other rights possible.

THE RIGHT TO DEFEND

Two of the rights we take for granted are the right to compel (i.e., subpoena) witnesses to come to court and the right to testify on our own behalf. A lawyer makes these rights a reality.

The power to ask for a subpoena assumes enough legal knowledge to use court procedures well before a trial. Likewise the defendant having the right to testify assumes that he will have a lawyer to question him. Both of these rights, however, were relatively late in coming.

Compulsion of Witnesses: In 1649 Lilburne wanted to subpoena witnesses:

"Subpoenas ... [some of my witnesses] are parliament men, and some of them officers of the army, and they will not come in without compulsion."[9]

As with his other pleas, Lilburne did not prevail.[10]

Although Lilburne could call witnesses, he could not subpoena them. Not until the end of the seventeenth century, with Parliament passing acts in 1696 and 1702, could a defendant compel witnesses to appear and have them sworn.[11]

This meant the prosecutor's sworn witnesses had more credibility than the defendant's. The antipathy of courts to allowing the defendant to subpoena witnesses had the same source as the rules preventing the defendant from testifying.

Titus Oates in the pillory

4. Langbein, *The Privilege*, at 1067 to 68, Langbein, *Before the Lawyers*, at 309; Fisher at 617 to 18.

5. The Treason Act of 1696 placed the accused and the crown on the same level. Lovell at 411.

6. See Kiralfy at 360 to 61.

7. Langbein, *Before the Lawyers*, at 309. As Langbein puts it, *"they legislated safeguards for themselves and left the underlings to suffer as before."*

8. Langbein, *Before the Lawyers*, at 309 to 10.

9. Quoted in Langbein, *The Privilege*, at 1056 (citing 4 State Trials at 1312). See also Wolfram at 238.

10. "Subpoena" is a noun from Latin meaning "under penalty," the first words of the writ (order) commanding the presence of someone under penalty of failure, from "*sub*" meaning "under" and "*poena*" meaning "penalty."

11. Fisher at 583, 597, 616. See also Langbein, *The Privilege*, at 1056. The reasoning behind the rule precluding not only defendants from testifying but also his witnesses was that felonies were capital and the system could not allow conflicting oaths with the death penalty. Thus not only could the defendant not testify under oath, Fisher at 598, his witnesses could not as well because of their bias to try to save him. *Id.* at 598 to 99 (citing Gilbert).

Westen cites Parliamentary acts in 1589 and 1606 giving the accused a limited right to call witnesses to testify but notes the accused still did not have the right to compel witnesses or to have them sworn. See Westen at 84 to 85, 87, 90 (noting that this was a key goal of Lilburne's Levellers).

Defendants Testifying: During medieval compurgation trials, the defendant took an oath. A compurgation trial, however, is about the oath, not the testimony, because the oath was the evidence.[1] Thus, before the sixteenth century the defendant could give his oath. But from the sixteenth to the nineteenth centuries, courts precluded the defendant from doing so, although he could give the jury his statement.[2]

The reason for the change was that the oath had become not just the evidence but instead the foundation for testimony. This created the potential for conflict because, unlike a medieval compurgation trial, there could now be conflicting testimony, meaning conflicting oaths. Both society and the criminal justice system could not accept the possibility of conflicting oaths because the oath legitimated the system.

Thus a rule developed in evidence law precluding a party from testifying on his own behalf. The party's interest in the outcome was a temptation for perjury and would therefore undermine the old system of oaths.[3]

This "party witness rule" was to protect the oath;[4] making classes of witnesses not competent to testify and prevented them from facing the temptation to lie. This was a product of the fact that juries did not yet have their modern role of detecting lies.[5]

In addition, there was a more practical necessity for prosecutors. If the oath is the evidence rather than

---

1. When the oath itself is qualitative evidence a natural tendency arises to play a numbers game counting multiple oaths as multiple proofs. See John H. Wigmore, *Required Numbers of Witnesses; A Brief History of the Numerical System in England*, 15 HARV. L. REV. 83, 85 (1901 to 02); *See also* Fisher at 652 to 55. The origins for this concept are biblical. Wigmore at 85 n.1 (quoting *Deuteronomy* 17:6, 19:15; *Numbers* 35:30; *Matthew* 18:16; *2 Corinthians* 13:1; *1 Timothy* 5:19; *Hebrews* 10:28; *John* 8:17). From there, the notion moved into Roman and canon law, Wigmore at 84, and the English chancery courts. *Id.* at 99. Thus matters such as wills, originally subject to ecclesiastical or chancery court jurisdiction, have required numbers of witnesses even today. In the common law, however, the jurors themselves were the witnesses, accounting for why jurors still take oaths. Thus numerology never came into practice in the common-law courts with the exception of cases involving treason or perjury. In treason cases it was because of the politics involved, where the sovereign could all too easily justify executions on little or no evidence. *Id.* at 100. As for perjury, more than one witness is needed as a practical matter to overcome the defendant's false testimony. *Id.* at 106; Fisher at 701.

2. Robert Popper, *History and Development of the Accused's Right to Testify*, 1962 WASH. U. L.Q. 454; 464 to 65. *See also* Fisher at 596 to 97 (noting the oddity that a defendant could testify in misdemeanor and in civil cases at the time).
We call it a witness "stand" because in England the witness actually stands in a box to testify. In America the witness sits in the "stand."

3. For Blackstone's views on the exclusion of the infamous or interested witnesses, including defendants, see Popper at 456. The modern reaction to this rule can be seen in Federal Rule of Evidence 601, which provides that "*[e]very person is competent to be a witness except as otherwise provided in these rules or by statue.*" Moreover, Federal Rule of Evidence 603 requires a witness to take an "*oath or affirmation*" before testifying. These modern rules react to the older system protecting the oath itself. *See* Fisher at 591. Indeed, Roman and canon law barred testimony of any potential perjurers, including women (in some cases), slaves, and those below age fourteen. *Id.* at 642. Additionally, rules barred testimony from the insane, the infamous, paupers, infidels, criminals, and children. *Id.* at 590, 606, 625; Morrison at 585. Because Quakers would not take oaths, the system disqualified their testimony, Fisher at 643, 657, and Edward Coke stated that only Christians could testify because the oath had meaning only to them. *Id.* at 657.

4. James Oldham, *Truth-Telling in the Eighteenth-Century English Courtroom*, 12 LAW & HIST. REV. 95, 96, 107 (1994). Wigmore traced the party disqualification rule to the distinction between the common-law jury trial and the wager of law (i.e., compurgation). See Joel N. Bodansky, *The Abolition of the Party-Witness Disqualification: An Historical Survey*, 70 KY. L.J. 91, 92 n.3 (1981 to 82). On the disqualification of interested parties, see Fisher at 657 and Q. Ullmann, *Medieval Principles of Evidence*, at 80 to 82. *See also* Westen at 86 (noting that the rationale was to avoid a "swearing match" because contradictory witnesses meant that someone committed perjury and the oath lost legitimacy).

the testimony, conflicting oaths would cancel each other, and the presumption of innocence would always mean no conviction.[6]

The party witness rule was rife with abuse, as Oates demonstrated. For one, it became clear that informants could testify under oath because they were not "parties" to the prosecution, despite the fact that they were paid for a conviction. Another anomaly of the party-witness disqualification rule was that codefendants tried separately could testify under oath for each other. But in a joint trial they could not do so unless they testified for the prosecution.[7]

Thus, the party-witness disqualification rule put the defendant at an unfair disadvantage.[8] The Stuart monarchs in particular were infamous for their use of perjurers to achieve state ends. The Treason Act of 1696, allowing defendants to testify under oath, came from this experience. Finally, conflicts between trial witnesses started to become a question of credibility rather than competence, and something for the jury to decide.[9]

In the context of the normal felony trial, however, the right of the defendant to testify under oath was a long time coming.[10] In the U.S., the first statute explicitly giving defendants this right was in 1864 in Maine.[11] In England, an 1898 statute gave the right.[12] Finally, the U.S. Supreme Court ruled in 1961 against any bar on the defendant testifying under oath.[13]

---

5. Fisher at 625 to 26.

6. Oldham at 103 (quoting Gilbert and noting that the lack of oath rendered the defendant's testimony the equivalent of hearsay and thus to be given less weight).

7. Popper at 457. Indeed the rule on codefendants not being allowed to testify in a joint trial lasted in England until the Statute of 1869. Id. at 469.

8. As Gilbert was to write, "*By the now Law in Cases of Treason the Witness against the King are admitted to their Oaths, because this [party disqualification rule] was abused in the late Reigns to derive a Credibility on the King's Witnesses as being upon Oath, tho' contradicted by Men of better Credit upon their Words only.*" Quoted in Fisher at 617.
See also Id. at 602 to 04 (stating how reforms were also a reaction to the Throckmorton trial of 1554). See also Popper at 456 to 57; Fisher at 617 to 18 (on reaction to Stuart perjurers); Id. at 607 to 08 (for the development of the two-witness rule for perjury and treason prosecutions). Regarding the Treason Act of 1696, see Langbein, The Privilage, at 1056. Of particular notoriety were the trials of Algeron Sydney and William Lord Russell.

9. Oldham at 98.
The law still gave presumptions to avoid direct conflicts between oaths. For instance, the so-called "rule of Bethel's case" determined that affirmative testimony was more credible than negative testimony. A basic rhetorical principle is that one cannot prove a negative, only a positive. The extension of this idea was that affirmative testimony was more truthful than negative testimony. For a complete accounting and survey of sources, see Fisher at 584, 597, 631 to 38.
Despite the best attempts of evidence experts and judges, the law could not avoid direct conflicts such as in the case of alibi defenses where one witness testifies the defendant was there and another that he was not. Id. at 648.

10. See Fisher at 581 n.9 (regarding secularization and democratization breaking down the oath system).

11. Fisher at 584.

12. Fisher at 662 (citing an Act to Amend the Law of Evidence, 61 & 62 Vict. Ch. 36 (1898)).

13. *Ferguson v. Georgia*, 365 U.S. 570, 593 (1961). Justice William J. Brennan gives an extensive historical account of the rule excluding defendants from testifying. See also *Rock v. Arkansas*, 483 U.S. 44, 51 to 53 (1987) (recognizing that defendants have an unconditional Sixth Amendment right to testify under oath).

But allowing testimony under oath breeds ethical dilemmas. ANATOMY OF A MURDER (Columbia Pictures 1959) is a realistic trial court drama directed by Otto Preminger and starring Jimmy Stewart as a small town lawyer and George C. Scott as the prosecutor, with Ben Gazzara as the defendant and Lee Remick as his wife. Real life lawyer Joseph Welch, who represented the U.S. Army in the McCarthy hearings, does a good turn as the judge. As the lawyers battle, Stewart's character is smart and works hard to keep the lines of his ethical conduct clear. See Richard Burst, *The 25 Greatest Legal Movies: Tales of Lawyers We've Loved and Loathed*, ABA JOURNAL Aug. 2008, at 41 (ranking *Anatomy of a Murder* as No. 4 on the list).

PROSECUTORS, REASONABLE DOUBT, AND THE PRESUMPTION OF INNOCENCE

Prosecutors: Though Lilburne complained of the injustice of not having a lawyer, the problem for most criminal defendants was that they did not have a prosecutor. If you have a prosecutor, the judge can leave the inquisitorial role. Plus, professional prosecutors, by definition, adhere to professional standards.[1]

From before Norman times, all prosecution was private.[2] The self-informed juror generally did not need a prosecutor.

For special cases, however, the king did have his own attorneys. The king had the "*praerogative*" (prerogative) of not having to appear himself in court. Thus, he sent an attorney, at first for specific cases in specific courts, but then generally to appear at any time in any court, that is, an "attorney general." By the seventeenth century these had become the offices of attorney general and solicitor general, and these were the first professional prosecutors.[3]

At the same time, the king's justices still had a prosecutorial function; remember, the king picked them to be law enforcement.[4] By Tudor times, the king's Justices of the Peace took over the pretrial case investigation for later presentation to the traveling justices

---

1. Hamilton Burger was the prosecutor in Perry Mason, who Perry dutifully beat every week. You have to wonder whether his character went home saying, *"Just once, I want to beat Perry Mason!"*

2. Danziger & Gillingham at 180.

3. Pound at 111 to 13.
These are offices today in the government of the United States. The **Attorney General** heads the Department of Justice and is the only member of the President's Cabinet who does not have the title of "secretary". The **Solicitor General** argues before the Supreme Court when the U.S. government is a party and answers to the Attorney General. As mentioned, he and his assistants argue Supreme Court cases wearing a morning coat.

U.S. Department of Justice Seal. Regarding the history of the Department of Justice seal and its meaning, see Rafael Alberto Madan, *The Sign and Seal of Justice*, 7 Ave Maria L. Rev. 123 (2008).

4. Glazebrook, at 583; Langbein, *Origins*, at 314 to 18.

5. The Office of Justice of the Peace grew out of the practice from the early 1200s where the king would appoint local knights to "*keep the king's peace*." "Justices of peace" started to get royal commissions under Edward II. Kynell at 156. Under Edward III these knights became regular officials with the name "justices of the peace." They could arrest and jail suspects and impose an early form of bond. Baker at 24 to 25. Early justices of the peace tried felonies but over time, they began to have a much more defined role in purely pretrial procedure. By the sixteenth century, they presided over only misdemeanor trials and the duties of arrest and detention. Langbein, *Origins*, at 319.

6. Langbein, *Origins*, at 320 to 23; Glazebrook at 584.

7. *See generally* Glazebrook; Langbein, *Origins*, at 313; Thompson I at 28 to 31. Justices of the Peace conducted an early form of the preliminary hearing. *Id.* at 319.
Justices of the Peace still exist today in many states, conducting preliminary hearings. Though modern criminal procedure and law constrains these Justices of the peace, the form is similar to the medieval period and they still "bind over" defendants for trial. Glazebrook at 584.
Judge Roy Bean (c. 1825 to 1903) is the most famous American Justice of the Peace. Although known as the "Hangin' Judge," there is no evidence he ever ordered an execution. Instead, he was an eccentric saloon keeper who posted signs proclaiming "Ice cold beer" and "Law west of the Pecos." He was first elected to office in 1884.

See The Life and Times of Judge Roy Bean (Cinerama Releasing 1972), directed by John Huston and staring Paul Newman.

from Westminster.[5] These Justices of the Peace had a specific role in bail decisions and an early type of subpoena power to investigate crime. This backed up private victims in their prosecutions.[6]

Under Queen Mary, Parliament passed several statutes from 1554 to 1555 defining the role of Justices of the Peace and in essence making them England's first prosecutor corps.[7] The Justices of the Peace served in this prosecutorial/inquisitorial role as an alternative to paid professional prosecutors well into the eighteenth century.[8] This prosecutorial function fit well with the Justices of the Peace's traditional role to keep the king's peace and make bail determinations.[9]

By the 1730s, things in England, especially London, began to change. Urbanization and population density pressured the older system of justice. Before professional police, "*thief takers*", who gained rewards for convictions, began to dominate criminal justice.[10] In various cases such as high treason, the crown employed attorneys. Now, different agencies of the government began to employ lawyers for prosecution.[11] The crown could no longer rely on the victim to prosecute crime.[12]

Prosecutors now had to prove the case with "reason" and evidence, overcoming "reasonable doubt."

Walter Brennan as Roy Bean, with Gary Cooper

The Westerner (Samuel Goldwyn 1940), directed by William Wyler, starred Gary Cooper and Walter Brennan, who won his record-setting third Best-Supporting Actor Oscar playing Judge Roy Bean.

8. Langbein, *Before the Lawyers*, at 282. See Bruce P. Smith, *The Emergence of Public Prosecution in London, 1790 to 1850*, 18 Yale J.L. & Human. 29, 33 (2006) (discussing the summary proceedings in police offices that dispensed with the need for victim participation in prosecution).

9. Glazebrook at 585.

10. See Beattie at 234; Fisher at 647; Landsman, *Contentious Spirit* at 572. We would call these "*thief takers*" "bounty hunters." But unlike modern bounty hunters who chase known felons and give them to the police, *thief takers* notoriously hauled anyone, usually the poor, to court and secured their conviction (and reward) with their own perjured testimony. There were no police forces, prosecutors, or defense attorneys to check them. And no *thief taker* could have been as cool as Steve McQueen in *Wanted: Dead or Alive* (CBS, from 1958 to 1961). *See also Dog the Bounty Hunter* (A&E, from August 31, 2004 to the present).

11. *See* Beattie at 221 to 22, 225 (noting the appearance of lawyers in court records in the 1720s and 1730s and specifically under the reign of George I).

12. *See generally* John H. Langbein, *The Prosecutorial Origins of Defense Counsel in the Eighteenth Century: The Appearance of Solicitors*, 58 Cambridge L.J. 314 (1999). Langbein, *The Privilege*, at 1070 describes the growth of professional prosecution through the 1770s and 1780s.

Reasonable Doubt:

Lilburne complained bitterly and often about his lack of trial rights. But somewhat offsetting this was a very high burden of proof. Judges held themselves and the prosecution, whether victims or lawyers, to the standard of proof *"clearer than noon day,"* which Lilburne's prosecutor argued:

Attorney General: *"You have heard the several charges proved unto you; for my part, I think it as clear as noon day."*[1]

This high standard of proof is part of the justification for denying the accused a lawyer.[2]

This *"clear as the light of noon day"* standard was a mainstay of medieval law, with origins from canon and Roman law.[3] It was also articulated as the *"any doubt"* standard. Thus jurors were to acquit if they had any doubts. Under medieval law an oath in a compurgation trial or trial by ordeal could defeat reason under the "any doubt" standard.

For prosecution, the balance was this: though the accused did not have the right to representation, subpoena power, the indictment, or to testify under oath, the prosecutor had the entire burden of proof *"beyond any doubt"*— not just the modern standard of proof *"beyond a reasonable doubt."*[4]

But just as professional prosecutors came on the scene, the intellectual foundation of England was changing. The seventeenth century was the Age of Reason.[5] Part of this was the "scientific revolution," stressing a rational approach to observation

---

1. *Quoted in* Wolfram at 243
The burden of proof was solely on the crown, thus eliminating the need, theoretically, for the defendant to provide any evidence to rebut the prosecution. Lovell at 150. As discussed above, the defendant was supposed to rely on the court to safeguard his legal interests. Westen at 86.

2. For example, **Chief Justice Sir William Scroggs** said to the Popish Plot defendants that *"the proof belongs to [the crown] to make out these intrigues of yours; therefore you need not have counsel, because the proof must be plain upon you, and then it will be in vain to deny the conclusion."* Quoted in Langbein, *Before the Lawyers*, at 308.

3. Richard M. Fraher, *Conviction According to Conscience: The Medieval Jurists' Debate Concerning Judicial Discretion and the Law of Proof*, 7 Law & Hist. Rev. 23, 23 to 24, 42 (1989); Anthony Morano, *A Reexamination of the Development of the Reasonable Doubt Rule*, 55 B.U. L. Rev. 507, 509 (1975) (outlining Roman and canon law origins).

To meet this standard, Roman and canon law (the *ius commune*) require proof by two unimpeachable witnesses or by confession.

Thus because of the exacting standard of proof, the confession became all-important. To get it, torture became a practice.

The rules for torture, however, were exacting. Also, the defendant had to repeat the confession freely in open court. If not, the court suppressed the statement.

4. Coke articulated *"the testimonies and the proofs of the offense ought to be so clear and manifest, as there can be no defense of it . . ."* Edward Coke, The Third Part of the Institute of the Law of England: Concerning High Treason and Other Pleas of the Crown in Criminal Causes 29 (London M. Flesher 1644). See Moreno at 512 (for discussion of Coke and the any doubt standard).

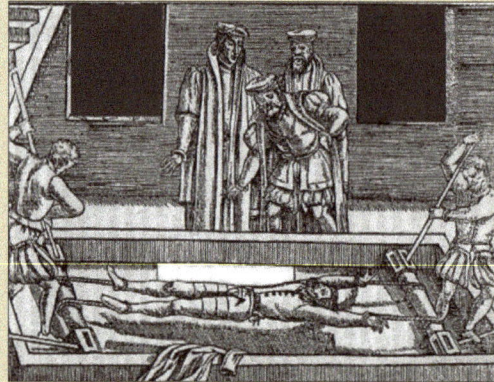

5. The **Age of Reason** was a period of seventeenth century Western history in which modern philosophy emerged and departed significantly from medieval scholasticism. The Age of Reason was after the Renaissance and before of the Enlightenment (or it was the earlier part of the Enlightenment). It marked a return to classical logic and the scientific method began in the classical era (ancient Greece and Rome) and reborn in the Renaissance.

and a logical/reasonable method for determining and explaining nature. This thinking influenced criminal procedure.[6] Methodology and reason became the standard for decision making rather than "irrational proofs."[7]

In 1756, Geoffrey Gilbert published one of the earliest works on evidence. He started it by discussing the nature of human reasoning and abstracting John Locke's *An Essay Concerning Human Understanding*,[8] marking the first effort to connect the law of proof with a methodology for decisionmaking. In this, Locke and Gilbert depart from medieval thought and jumped back to Aristotle's discussion of proof:

"[I]t is evidently equally foolish to accept probable reasoning from a mathematician and to demand from a rhetorician scientific proofs."[9]

Aristotle's point, which Locke and Gilbert echo, is that the nature of proof in science is different than other human endeavors. For the rhetorician, including the players in a system of criminal justice, a rational approach is to accept *"probable reasoning,"* not absolute proof *"beyond all doubt."* Proof *"beyond a reasonable doubt,"* the modern standard, must do.[10]

To establish this proof the best evidence is necessary but not absolute evidence, which is rarely present.[11] This freed the common-law jury system from the inquisitorial obsession with extraction of confessions to prove a criminal case.

The School of Athens by Raphael (1509 to 10)

Although created in the Renaissance, the painting shows the dawn of the Age of Reason.

John Locke

Aristotle, a detail of Rafael's *The School of Athens*. Aristotle gestures to the earth and his belief in knowledge through empirical observation and experience, while holding a copy of his *Nicomachean Ethics*.

6. See BARBARA J. SHAPIRO, "BEYOND REASONABLE DOUBT" AND "PROBABLE CAUSE" 7 (1991).

7. Anti-Catholicism drove much of this change in thinking. Theodore Waldman, *Origins of the Legal Doctrine of Reasonable Doubt*, 20 J. HIST. IDEAS 299, 300 to 01 (1959). "*Moral certainty*" became the standard that scientists, philosophers, and religious thinkers used to distinguish themselves from "*irrational*" Catholics. Waldman at 303, 310; SHAPIRO at 7, 19.

8. Waldman at 305 to 06, 311; Morano at 513 to 14. *See also* SHAPIRO at 8, 11, 17, 18, 25, 26; Michael MacNair, *Sir Jeffrey Gilbert and His Treatises*, 15 LEGAL HIST. 252, 256 (1994).

9. Waldman at 306, *quoting* ARISTOTLE, ETHICA NICOMACHEA bk. 10, Ch. 3, (W. David Ross trans., Oxford Univ. Press, 1925).

10. In tort and civil law, this leads to the "reasonable man" standard. Waldman at 311, 315 to 16.

11. Waldman at 313. Evidence law does, of course, employ the higher standard of "*scientific proof*," especially relating to expert testimony. Federal Rules of Evidence 702 and 703. However, it is still the jury using Aristotle's "*probable reasoning*" that decides the case.

Professional prosecutors, who arrived just as beliefs about the nature of proof were changing, pushed for the *"reasonable doubt"* standard. The prosecutor had to introduce only certain kinds of logical proof but no longer proof *"clear as the noon day"* or *"beyond any doubt."*[1] Thus the push for the *"beyond a reasonable doubt"* standard decreased the prosecutor's burden.

But despite the decrease from *"beyond all doubt"* to *"beyond a reasonable doubt,"* one thing never changed in the common law: the prosecutor had the burden of proof because the defendant was presumed innocent.[2]

The Presumption of Innocence: About the same time courts were figuring out *"beyond a reasonable doubt,"* Justice William Blackstone in 1769 wrote that

"the law holds that it is better that ten guilty persons escape than that one innocent suffer."[3]

This statement to describe the presumption of innocence is called *"Blackstone's formulation"* or the *"Blackstone ratio."* But though Blackstone gets the credit, the idea was hardly original to him.[4]

In *Genesis*, Abraham reminds God of the presumption of innocence when God was going to destroy Sodom and Gomorrah for their *"wickedness"*:

"Will you sweep away the righteous with the wicked?"

Certainly God, Abraham beseeches, would not ignore the presumption of innocence:

"Far be it for you to do such a thing—to kill the righteous with the wicked, treating the righteous and the wicked alike. Far be it for you! Will not the Judge of all the earth do right?"[5]

God agrees that if there are fifty good people he will spare the cities. Abraham

---

1. Morano at 508, 514. See SHAPIRO at 21 for a contrary view and the prosecutorial origins of the *"reasonable doubt"* standard. Shapiro argues that the older standard incorporating the term *"moral certainty"* encompassed the *"reasonable doubt"* standard.

Blackstone

2. *Coffin v. United States*, 156 U.S. 432, 453 (1895) (*"The principle that there is a presumption of innocence in favor of the accused is the undoubted law, axiomatic and elementary, and its enforcement lies at the foundation of the administration of our criminal law."*).

3. 4 BLACKSTONE, COMMENTARIES ON THE LAWS OF ENGLAND *358 (1st ed. 1769).

4. Coffin at 456, quoting from Lord Gillies in the English *McKinley's* case (1817), 33 St. Tr. 275, 596, that *"this presumption [of innocence] is to be found in every code of law which has reason, and religion, and humanity, for a foundation. It is a maxim which ought to be inscribed in indelible characters in the heart of every judge and juryman."*

Despite this nice pronouncement, all governments have not universally followed it. German chancellor Otto von Bismarck, for example, supposedly remarked that *"it is better that ten innocent men suffer than one guilty man escape."* Quoted in Alexander Volokh, n Guilty Men, 146 U. PENN. L. REV. 173, 195 (1997), available at http://www.law.ucla.edu/volokh/guilty.htm (last visited

Otto von Bismarck (1815 to 1898) was a Prussian/German statesman of the late nineteenth century.

Oct. 8, 2010). But if Otto is correct, and the presumption of innocence is not universal, then out the door goes PRESUMED INNOCENT (Warner Brothers 1990) from Scott Turow's novel of the same name (1987).

5. *Genesis* 18:20 to 32.

6. See Volokh at 173 to 74 (discussing God and Abraham and tracing the concept of the ratio of guilty to innocent from ancient times through the present).

The Destruction of Sodom.

eventually plea bargains this down to ten *"righteous"* people:

"And he said, Oh let not the Lord be angry, and I will speak yet but this once: Peradventure ten shall be found there. And God said, I will not destroy it for ten's sake."

Presumably Sodom and Gomorrah had many hundred wicked inhabitants who were all going to "beat the rap" to save just ten—much better than Blackstone's ratio of ten to one.[6] Of course, Abraham may not have made a very good deal because God, being God, already knew there would not be ten good people in the cities and smote them anyway.[7]

Ancient Greek law in both Athens and Sparta incorporated the presumption of innocence.[8] It also was a key part of Roman law

"that no man should be condemned on a criminal charge in his absence, because it was better to let the crime of a guilty person go unpunished than to condemn the innocent."[9]

The Emperor Julian once sat as a judge where a prosecutor who could not beat the presumption of innocence declared "Oh, illustrious Caesar! if it is sufficient to deny, what hereafter will become of the guilty?"

Julian replied:

"If it suffices to accuse, what will become of the innocent?"[10]

Roman law combined with the biblical precedent for the presumption of innocence and passed into the church's canon law.[11] It remained the standard of church court procedure throughout the Middle Ages and even applied in heresy trials, although other heresy inquisition procedures, such as torture, negated it.

---

7. But God did save Abraham's nephew, Lot. The homosexual practices of Sodom give us our modern term "sodomy."

As for playing God with the presumption of innocence, see Minority Report (DreamWorks and 20th Century Fox 2002), which shows a science fiction world of 2054 were police, with the help of clairvoyants, arrest criminals *before* they commit the crime.

8. *Coffin*, 156 U.S. at 454 (outlining secondary sources).

9. Quoted in *Coffin*, 156 U.S. at 454 (citing letter from Trajan to Julius Frontonus; Dig. L. XLVIII, tit. 19, 1. 5). The Supreme Court in *Coffin* went on to quote from Roman law as follows: "In all cases of doubt, the most merciful construction of facts should be preferred." Dig. L. L, Tit. XVII, 1. 56.

In criminal cases the milder construction shall always be preserved." Dig. L. L, Tit. XVII, 1. 155, s. 2. "In cases of doubt it is no less just than it is safe to adopt the milder construction." Dig. L. L, Tit. XVII, 1. 192, s. 1.

Julian (331/332 A.D.–363 A.D.)

Emperor Trajan

10. Quoted in *Coffin*, 156 U.S. at 455 (citing Rerum Gestarum, L. XVIII, c. 1).

Fragment of *The Justice of Trajan* by Delacroix (1840) showing Trajan taking time out from the Dacian Wars to hear the case of a mother whose son was murdered.

11. *Coffin*, 156 U.S. at 455 (citing Decretum Gratiani de Presumptionibus, L. II, T. XXIII, c. 14, AD 1198; [***492] Corpus Juris Canonici Hispani et Indici, R.P. Murillo Velarde, Tom. 1, L. II, n.140; Kenneth Pennington, *Innocent until Proven Guilty: The Origins of a Legal Maxim,* cited in Patricia M. Dugan, The Penal Process and the Protection of Rights in Canon Law (2005); see also Ullmann, *The Defense of the Accused* at 486.

The presumption of innocence then passed from canon and Roman law to England.[1] In the ninth century, King Alfred hanged a judge who had executed a defendant

"when the jurors were in doubt about their verdict, for in cases of doubt one should rather save than condemn."[2]

By 1471, English Chief Justice John Fortescue declared that

"one would much rather that twenty guilty persons should escape the punishment of death than that one innocent person should be condemned and suffer capitally."[3]

Fortescue provides double Blackstone's ratio: twenty to one rather than ten to one.

Two hundred years later in 1678, however, Lord Chief Justice Matthew Hale defined the presumption of innocence as follows:

"In some cases presumptive evidence goes far to prove a person guilty, though there be no express proof of the fact to be committed by him, but then it must be very warily pressed, for it is better five guilty persons should escape unpunished than one innocent person should die."[4]

Thus Hale's ratio is five to one, only half of Blackstone's.

Maybe Blackstone took

---

1. *Coffin*, 156 U.S. at 455. See also Ullmann, *Some Medieval Principles of Criminal Procedure*; Anthony Morano, *A Reexamination of the Development of the Reasonable Doubt Rule*, 55 B.U. L. Rev. 507, 509 (1975).

2. Discussed in Volokh at 182. Volokh also mentions King Æthelred the Unready providing that twelve *thanes* (knights) and a representative of the king would swear upon a relic that they would "accuse no innocent man, nor conceal any guilty one."

3. *Coffin*, 156 U.S. 432 at 455, *quoting* Fortescue and *citing* De Laudibus Legum Angliae, (Amos trans, Cambridge Univ. Press, 1825). For Fortescue's comment on the jury's role in the presumption of innocence, see **The Seventh Amendment**, in this series.

4. *Coffin*, 156 U.S. at 456 *quoting* Matthew Hale and *citing* 1 Hale P.C. 24 and 2 Hale P.C. 290.

5. Quoted in Volokh at 186. Despite this, Increase could never bring himself to decry what happened during the Salem witch trials.

6. Quoted in Volokh at 175.

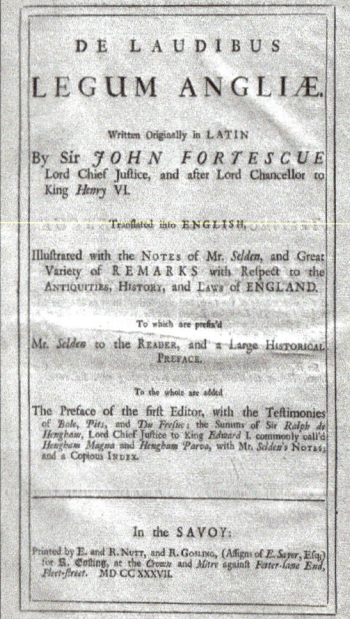

Increase Mather

Benjamin Franklin

the writings of his two illustrious predecessors and just split the difference to come up with his famous ten to one ratio.

In America, just under eighty years before Blackstone, Increase Mather on October 3, 1692, wrote that even with witches

"it were better that Ten Suspected Witches should escape, than that the Innocent Person should be Condemned." [5]

Although Benjamin Franklin was Blackstone's contemporary and certainly read him, he articulated the ratio in much grander terms: better that one hundred guilty persons *"escape than that one innocent Person should suffer."* [6] Thus Franklin advocated ten times Blackstone's ratio.

However we express the ratio—5:1, 10:1, 20:1, or 100:1—it still raises the question of how much

people, that is, modern jurors, actually believe that a defendant is innocent at the start of a trial.[7] In hundreds of courtrooms every day judges tell juries that defendants are *"presumed innocent"* and that prosecutors must prove their case *"beyond a reasonable doubt."*

But although we take this law for granted, the first time it all came together was in the Boston Massacre trial.

Carl Bett as Judd

Barry Newman as Petrocelli

7. Who Killed Perry Mason? Every week for decades Perry Mason defended innocent clients. Later, *Matlock* carried on the formula with a folksy twist. In *Judd, for the Defense* (ABC, 1967 to 69), Clinton Judd defend innocent people and the social issues of the day. In the 1970's, *Owen Marshall: Counselor at Law* (ABC, 1971 to 74) defended the innocent along with his assistant Lee Majors, who became television's *The Six Million Dollar Man*. *The Bold Ones: The Lawyers* (NBC, 1968 to 72) featured Burl Ives as respected attorney Walter Nichols who hired two young brothers (Joseph Campanella and James Farentino) to defend the innocent. In *Petrocelli* (NBC, 1974 to 76), the client was certain to be convicted until Petrocelli would get evidence suggesting, but not necessarily proving, an alternative possibility, which the jury would accept as a reasonable doubt under the presumption of innocence.

But these shows are decades old. Today, the few television shows about criminal defense attorneys are edgy, such as *The Practice* (20 Century Fox TV, 1997 to 2004), with, more often than not, guilty clients providing the drama. Prosecutors now rule the television legal drama. *Law and Order* and its numerous spin-offs present the prosecutor putting away the guilty against the odds. Forget Blackstone's ratio; there are no innocents in the *Law and Order* world, and acquittals are miscarriages of justice. The *Law and Order* franchise, as well as semi-news shows like *Nancy Grace* (HLN, February 21, 2005 to present), represent an entire industry based on the presumption of guilt. Although not about lawyers, the reality show *COPS* (Fox, 1989 to present), which follows police officers around with cameras as they arrest suspects red handed, starts with the statement *"COPS is filmed on location as it happens. All suspects are considered innocent until proven guilty in a court of law."* The message: all defendants are guilty, and the presumption of innocence just gets in the way.

Arthur Will as Owen Marshall

Image by Helen Koop

THE BOSTON MASSACRE TRIAL

The Boston Massacre trial of 1770 is our first record of the prosecution arguing for the *"beyond a reasonable doubt"* standard.[1]

On March 5, 1770, British soldiers in Boston faced an unruly crowd. After provocation, or without any reason at all (depending on whose side you read), the soldiers fired into the crowd, killing five people.[2]

At the murder trials in late 1770, Captain Thomas Preston and eight soldiers were represented by John Adams, a future signer of the Declaration of Independence and second American president.[3] Prosecuting the case for the crown was Robert Treat Paine, another future signer of the Declaration.[4]

Adams gave a passionate closing argument that the jury should acquit if they had *"any doubt"*:

"[T]he best rule in doubtful cases, is, rather to incline to acquittal than conviction: and . . . [w]here you are doubtful never act; that is, if you doubt of the prisoner's guilt, never declare him guilty; this is always the rule, especially in cases of life."[5]

Adams articulated the presumption of innocence.

Paine argued from the perspective of the Age of Reason:

"Our law in General that it is Ultima Ratio the last improvement of Reason which in the nature of it will not admit any Proposition to be true of which it has not Evidence . . ."[6]

A medieval lawyer or judge would never have made such a statement. But Paine builds on Locke and

---

1. Morano at 508. The somewhat later Irish Treason trials of 1798 are another possible source. *See id.* J.W. May, *Some Rules of Evidence: Reasonable Doubt in Civil and Criminal Cases*, 10 Am. L. Rev. 642 (1876); 9 J. Wigmore, Evidence § 2497 (3d ed. 1940); C. McCormick, Law of Evidence § 341 (2d ed. 1972). Langbein, *Before the Lawyers*, at 266 (citing McCormick, states that the "reasonable doubt" standard did not develop until the nineteenth century). Shapiro at 22 to 23, however, agrees with the Morano view that the Boston Massacre trials were first.

Crispus Attucks

2. This included Crispus Attucks, the first black man to die for American Independence.
  For the record of the Boston Massacre trial with speeches and testimony, see the Boston Historical Society site, http://www.bostonmassacre.net/trial/index.htm (last visited June 13, 2007).
  For the propaganda effect of the massacre and trial, see Arthur Schlesinger, Prelude to Independence: The Newspaper War on Britain, 1764 to 1776 (1958).

Paul Revere's illustration of the Boston Massacre

The Boston Massacre

3. John Adams. Also for the defense was Josiah Quincy, Jr. Regarding Josiah Quincy, see Daniel R. Coquillette, *The Legal Education of a Patriot: Josiah Quincy Jr.'s Law Commonplace (1763)*, 39 Ariz. St. L.J. 317 (2007).

Boston Massacre trial bill

4. Robert Treat Paine later served as Massachusetts's first attorney general (1777 to 90) and as a state supreme court judge (1790 to 1804).
  Paine was assisted by Samuel Quincy, see Morano at 516 to 17, who was Josiah Quincy's brother. The Revolutionary War separated the two. Samuel Quincy was a Loyalist and left America forever in 1776.

Robert Treat Paine

Samuel Quincy

Gilbert's foundation to argue that doubts had to be reasonable:

"[I]f therefore in the examination of this Cause the Evidence is not sufficient to Convince you beyond a reasonable Doubt of the Guilt of all . . . you will acquit them, but if the Evidence be sufficient to convince you of their Guilt beyond a reasonable Doubt the Justice of the Law will require you to declare them Guilty . . . ."[7]

The judges were split on jury instructions. Senior Judge Edmund Trowbridge charged the jury with the "*any doubt*" standard.[8]

In the end, Adams won. Captain Preston was acquitted, and the jury found only two of his men, Hugh Montgomery and Mathew Kilroy, guilty of manslaughter. Their punishment was branding on the thumb with a hot iron after receiving "*benefit of clergy.*"[9]

But despite Adams's successful assertion of the "*any doubt*" standard, it was the "reasonable doubt" standard that became our standard today. Perhaps this was in some part a reaction to the perceived leniency of the Boston Massacre trials. Thus what was the prosecutor's innovation to lessen the "*any doubt*" standard became the defendant's primary protection from an erroneous conviction.[10]

As the Boston Massacre trials illustrate, prosecutors were now facing defendants with trial rights, including the right to defense counsel, like John Adams.[11] But how did the process get from Lilburne, who did not get a lawyer despite his pleas, to Adams, and on to the Sixth Amendment guarantee of the defendant's right to the "*Assistance of Counsel for his defense*"?

---

5. *Quoted in* Morano at 517.

6. *Quoted in* Morano at 517.

7. *Quoted in* Morano at 517.

8. Morano at 517 to 18. In addition to Trowbridge and Oliver, Supreme Court Justice John Cushing and Superior Court Judge Benjamin Lynde presided over the trials. *Id.* at 517.
  Interestingly, Justice Peter Oliver agreed with the crown, telling the jury "*if upon the whole, ye are in any reasonable doubt of their guilt, ye must then, agreeable to the rule of law, declare them innocent.*" He was a Loyalist, and his family were bitter business and political rivals of James Otis and Samuel Adams. He served as Chief Justice of Massachusetts from 1772 until deposed by Revolutionists in 1775. After leaving America during the Revolution, he never returned.

Peter Oliver

9. "Benefit of clergy" had passed into the common law as a basis for granting leniency. For example, instead of being hanged, a first-time offender convicted of manslaughter would receive the "burnt in the hand" punishment of a branded "M" for "manslayer." Originally this was to stop clerics from invoking the benefit more than once. Congress abolished benefit of clergy in 1790 though it survived in some states and may even remain technically available today. The British Parliament did not abolish benefit of clergy until 1827. See Jeffrey K. Sawyer, *Benefit of Clergy in Maryland and Virginia*, 34 Am. J. Legal Hist. 49 (1990).

10. Morano at 519. *See In re* Winship, 397 U.S. 358, 361 to 64, and 369 to 72 (1970) (Harlan, J., concurring).

11. John Adams argued during the trial, "*if I can but be the instrument of preserving one life, his blessing and tears of transport shall be a sufficient consolation to me for the contempt of all mankind.*" Quoted in Deborah A. Schwartz & Jay Wishingard, *The Eighth Amendment, Beccaria, and the Enlightenment: An Historical Justification for Weems v. United States Excessive Punishment Doctrine*, 24 Buff. L. Rev. 781, 814 (1975).

John Adams

THE AVERAGE GUY'S TRIAL IN ENGLAND AND AMERICA

We Americans have the idea that all our great rights came from England and our job is to "preserve" the ancient customs and liberties. The American Revolution perpetuated this idea that we just wanted our *"rights as Englishmen."*

But America was the product of progressive Enlightenment thought. In many areas the colonists were more advanced in the concept of rights than the English. As the Boston Massacre trials demonstrated, this was especially true regarding the rights of the accused.[1]

The American Bill of Rights reflected a broader concept of liberty, giving status to a defendant's criminal and procedural rights unavailable in Britain.[2]

England versus America: The trial of the average Englishman, especially if he was poor, would have been much like the *"altercation"* of Queen Elizabeth's time. Existing records show a trial that lasted about half an hour, with the judge doing the direct and cross-examination.[3] The accused defended himself and was expected to tell his side of the events. His statement could exonerate or hang him.[4]

His trial was adversarial in that it was public, with witnesses and direct confrontation. The main adversaries were the judge and/or witnesses. Not until the eighteenth century did the trial became adversarial in the sense of a contest between a prosecutor and defense attorney.[5]

As discussed, by the mid-1700s, professional prosecutors started to appear as a matter of course. In response, any defendant who could sought counsel. Counsels' advocacy, by modern standards, was limited, as the following statement from a judge to a defendant in a trial at the Old Bailey in 1777 demonstrates:

"Your counsel are not at liberty to state any matter of fact;

---

1. Randolph N. Jonakait, *The Rise of the American Adversary System: America before England*, 14 WIDENER L. REV. 323 (2009) (noting that *"America moved to a full adversary system before England."*).

2. The English Bill of Rights only has statutory status, and the English wrote in using the phrase *"ought not"* instead of the "American Bill of Rights" *"shall not."* WILTSHIRE at 98.

3. BAKER at 510; Beattie at 221 to 22. *See also* Klerman at 135, 145 (regarding the judge's quasi-prosecutorial role). Regarding judicial power in the colonies, see William E. Nelson, *Government by Judiciary: The Growth of Judicial Power in Colonial Pennsylvania*, 59 SMU L. REV. 3 (2006).

4. Langbein, *The Privilege*, at 1053 to 54. Langbein notes that any real right to silence would not occur until much later with the advent of defense lawyers in the late 1800s.

5. *See generally* Langbein, *Before the Lawyers*, and John H. Langbein, *Shaping the Eighteenth-Century Criminal Trial: A View from the Ryder Sources*, 50 U. CHI. L. REV. 1 (1983). For Langbein's definition of the phrase *"the accused speaks trial,"* see Langbein, *Before the Laweyrs*, at 283. *See also* Landsman at 1 (extensively documented demonstration from the Old Bailey session papers of the development during the 1700s of the adversary trial and the transfer of the adversarial parts from judges to lawyers). *See also* Stephan Landsman, *From Gilbert to Bentham: The Reconceptualization of Evidence Theory*, 36 WAYNE L. REV. 1149 (1990) (outlining this same change by analyzing evidence scholars from Gilbert to Bentham).

6. Langbein, *The Privilege*, at 1054. *See also* Beattie at 226, 231 to 32. The Old Bailey is the central criminal court in London (a *"bailey"* is part of a castle), dealing with major criminal cases. It stands on the site of the medieval Newgate Gaol. For records, see http://www.oldbaileyonline.org.

The Old Bailey is often a feature in literature and film: Charles Dickens, in A TALE OF TWO CITIES, has Charles Darnay's treason trial at the Old Bailey. Sir John Mortimer used his own experience at the Old Bailey to create the fictional character Horace Rumpole, alias *Rumpole of the Bailey* (BBC, 1975 to 92). V in the graphic novel V FOR VENDETTA (Quality Comics (U.K.) and Vertigo/DC Comics (U.S.A.) 1982 to 88) and its film adaptation, V FOR VENDETTA (Warner Brothers 2006), blows up the Old Bailey.

An Old Bailey trial around 1808

they are permitted to examine your witnesses; and they are here to speak to any matters of law that may arise; but if your defense arises out of a matter of fact, you must yourself state it to me and the jury."[6]

Thus the defendant had to speak for himself, and defense counsel could not even give the jury a closing argument.[7] The lawyer could examine defense witnesses and argue points of law, but little else.[8]

But defense lawyers were at least there. Although they could not cross-examine witnesses, they did object to evidence. Over time these objections developed into arguments, questioning witnesses, and a form of cross-examination.[9]

In America, however, it appears that defense counsel were not just at the trial but participating in a fully developed adversarial system. This was certainly true by the Boston Massacre trial, where Adams argued to the jury after having cross-examined prosecution witnesses.

Thus the Sixth Amendment does not reflect the *"rights of Englishmen"* but of Americans. The First Congress, while arguing the Bill of Rights, passed the Sixth Amendment with almost no debate.[10] Americans knew well the history of Throckmorton and Raleigh, the Star Chamber cases against the Puritans, and the abusive prosecution of the "popish plotters."[11]

The Aaron Burr treason trial reflects the broad scope of the trial rights the Sixth Amendment articulates. Chief Justice John Marshall was prepared to allow Burr to subpoena President Thomas Jefferson or Jefferson's letter to his attorney general.[12] A defendant had no such right in England at the time.

The Sixth Amendment shows that by the end of the eighteenth century, America did not simply adopt England's adversary system but instead developed trial procedures independently and in advance of England.[13]

---

7. Langbein, *Before the Lawyers*, at 313. Part of this older type of trial lives on today in the defendant's allocution rights at sentencing. Also, under the U.S. military's procedure the accused may at sentencing make a sworn or unsworn statement. R.C.M. 1001(c)(2). The same is true at a pretrial investigation (the equivalent of a bind-over hearing). See R.C.M. 405 (f)(7), (11), and (12). Manual for Courts-Martial, United States (2008).

William Garrow

8. In America, though, the defendant shall *"have the Assistance of Counsel for his defense."* as guaranteed in the Sixth Amendment. In England these rights were not formally guaranteed until the Prisoner's Counsel Act of 1836. Beattie at 250.

9. Beattie at 233; Langbein, *Before the Lawyers*, at 311. See also Landsman, *Contentions Spirit* at 512 (regarding the growth of lawyer cross-examination).
For an interesting account of a criminal defense lawyer of that time named William Garrow, see Beattie at 236; also Beattie n.14 for an accounting of lawyer fees.

10. Westen at 74.

11. Westen at 94.

12. Westen at 101 to 08. Burr ended up dropping his request, went to trial without it, and was acquitted.

13. Jonakait at 323. Jonakait extensively reviewed court records of colonial and early republic New Jersey and New York to conduct a detailed statistical analysis. He then compared this with Langbein's work on trials in England to note the difference in procedure and rights of the accused. For a brief history of lawyers in the colonies before the American Revolution, see Pound at 130 to 74.

Garrow cross examining

Americans had fully developed systems of public prosecution. The defendant could compel witnesses to testify and could testify under oath.[1]

And he had the right to a lawyer, an especially important right because with a lawyer the defendant can assert all his other trial rights.[2]

LILBURNE'S LAWYER

In the end, Lilburne never got the lawyer that "*common equity and justice*" should have given him. But his legacy is our Sixth and Fifth Amendments' guarantee of a lawyer.[3]

Because a lawyer does the talking, you have the right

---

1. *See generally* Jonakait.
   This means by the nineteenth century a young Abraham Lincoln could get his start as a lawyer in Springfield, Missouri, and go on to become president of the United States. Henry Fonda starred as YOUNG MR. LINCOLN (20th Century Fox 1939), a fictionalized biography-drama directed by John Ford. It centers on the murder trial and Lincoln's famous "*light of the silvery moon*" cross-examination. In the movie, the key witness is a friend of the victim who claims to have seen the murder at some distance under the light of the moon. Using an almanac, Lincoln demonstrated that on the night in question the moon could not have provided the light. He then drives the witness – Perry Mason like – to confess.
   YOUNG MR. LINCOLN depicts the real life 1858 murder trial of William "Duff" Armstrong. In defending Armstrong, Lincoln cross-examined witness Charles Allen on how he could have seen Armstrong strike the victim. Allen testified that he was at a distance of 150 feet but could clearly see by the light of the full moon. Using an almanac, Lincoln showed Allen lied because the moon on that night could not have given off enough light. Armstrong was acquitted. He died in 1899 and is buried in Mason County, Illinois His grave plaque reads, "WILLIAM DUFF ARMSTRONG, *accused slayer of Preston Metzker, May 7, 1858 freed by Lincoln in almanac trial.*"
   In 2003, the Library of Congress put YOUNG MR. LINCOLN on the National Film Registry for being "*culturally, historically, or aesthetically significant.*" The *ABA Journal* rates the film No. 23 in its Top 25 best lawyer films. *See* Richard Burst, *The 25 Greatest Legal Movies: Tales of Lawyers We've Loved and Loathed*, ABA JOURNAL, Aug. 2008, at 45.

Duff Armstrong's grave marker. Find a grave at http://image1.findagrave.com/photos/2008/206/28517102_121701050379.jpg (last visited Sept. 25, 2010).

Courtroom scene from YOUNG MR. LINCOLN showing that in early nineteenth century America, a defendant had his trial rights

2. From Atticus Finch, the lawyer we all want to be, to *L.A. Law*, the lawyers with the sex lives we all want to have.

Fonda as Lincoln

A Young Abe Lincoln

to silence.[4] A lawyer can cross-examine witnesses and prepare the case. He knows procedures and the law.[5] He can call prosecutors and even judges to account.

The lawyer gives the defendant the chance to defend.

But even in America the universality of this right was a long time coming. It was not until 1963 that the Supreme Court ruled that every defendant in a serious case must have a lawyer, even if he can not afford one himself.[6]

Today the right is a given.

Although Lilburne never got his lawyer, he did have one thing going for him. He had a jury.

L.A. Law was a television legal drama (NBC, 1986 to 1994). The fictional Los Angeles firm McKenzie, Brackman, Chaney, and Kuzak handled cases of abortion, racism, gay rights, homophobia, sexual harassment, AIDS, and domestic violence. And for law students of my generation, it was a must-see!

3. It never hurts to return to the actual words of the Sixth Amendment: *"and to have the Assistance of Counsel for his defense"*

The right to counsel from the Fifth Amendment comes in the context of the right to remain silent, which is meaningless without a lawyer to assert the defense. *But see* Berghuis v. Thompkins, 560 U.S. 370 (2010) (a suspect must expressly invoke his right to remain silent). Regarding the need of counsel for the right to remain silent, see Langbein, *The Privilege*, at 1048.

4. See *The Fifth Amendment*, in this series, published by Constitution Press, 2017

5. As the Supreme Court recognizes, the Sixth Amendment *"embodies a realistic recognition of the obvious truth that the average defendant does not have the professional legal skill to protect himself when brought before a tribunal with power to take his life or liberty..."* Johnson v. Zerbst, 304 U.S. 458, 462 to 63 (1938).

6. In June 1962, the Supreme Court agreed to review the felony conviction of a fifty-one-year-old drifter with an eighth grade education. Clarence Earl Gideon hand-wrote his petition from his Florida prison cell. *"The question is very simple. I requested the [trial] court to appoint me attorney and the court refused."* Future Justice Abe Fortas argued for Gideon.

Overturning precedent, the Court on March 18, 1963, unanimously reversed his conviction. *Gideon v. Wainwright*, 372 U.S. 335 (1963), remains the landmark case requiring that, under the Sixth Amendment, every defendant facing serious charges must have a lawyer. Five months after the Supreme Court ruling, Gideon was retried with a lawyer and acquitted.

Gideon died in 1972 and is buried in an unmarked grave in his hometown of Hannibal, Missouri George Hodak, ABA JOURNAL, Mar. 2009, at 72. The Florida Department of Corrections webpage features Gideon, ironic given that the case was against Florida. See http://www.dc.state.fl.us/oth/timeline/1963-1965.html (last visited July 8, 2007). See Paul M. Rashkind, *Gideon v. Wainwright: A 40th Birthday Celebration and the Threat of a Midlife Crisis*, FLA. B.D. 12 (Mar. 2003). *See* ANTHONY LEWIS, GIDEON'S TRUMPET (reissue ed. 1989), and the movie (1980) starring Henry Fonda as Clarence Earl Gideon. The title refers to the biblical Gideon, who ordered his small force to attack a larger enemy and won using trumpets as a trick. *Judges* 7:16 to 22.

Clarence Earl Gideon

Gideon's plea and handwritten petition to the Supreme Court

BIBLIOGRAPHY

CASES:
Berghuis v. Thompkins, 560 U.S. ___ (2010).
Coffin v. U.S., 156 U.S. 432 (1895).
Coy v. Iowa, 487 U. S. 1012 (1988).
Crawford v. Washington, 541 U.S. 36 (2004).
Gideon v. Wainwright, 372 U.S. 335 (1963).
Hamdi v. Rumsfeld, 542 U.S. 507 (2004).
In re Winship, 397 U.S. 358 (1970).
Johnson v. Zerbst, 304 U.S. 458 (1938).
Marbury v. Madision, 5 U.S. (1 Cranch) 137 (1803).
Miranda v. Arizona, 384 U.S. 436 (1966).
Rock v. Arkansas, 483 U.S. 44 (1987).

CONSTITUTIONS:
MASSACHUSETTS CONSTITUTION, Part The First, art. XXX (1780).
The DECLARATION OF INDEPENDENCE.
UNITED STATES CONSTITUTION.

STATUTES:
Federal Rules of Civil Procedure.
Habeas Corpus Act of 1679 *available at* http://press-pubs.uchicago.edu/founders/documents/a1_9_2s2.html (last visited February 26, 2008).
The County Courts Amendment Act, ending the Hundred Courts.

BOOKS:
4 BLACKSTONE COMMENTARIES ON THE LAWS OF ENGLAND (1st ed. 1769).
8 WIGMORE, EVIDENCE (3d ed. 1940).
A.E. DICK HOWARD, MAGNA CARTA: TEXT AND COMMENTARY (1964).
A.K.R. KIRALFY, POTTER'S HISTORICAL INTRODUCTION TO ENGLISH LAW (4th ed. 1958).
ALEXANDRE DUMAS, THE THREE MUSKETEERS (1844).
ALISON WEIR, QUEEN ISABELLA (2005).
ANTHONY LEWIS, GIDEON'S TRUMPET (Reissue ed. 1989).
ANTONIA FRASER, THE LIVES OF THE KINGS AND QUEENS OF ENGLAND (1975).
ARISTOTLE, ETHICS (Penguin Classics ed. 1955).
ARTHUR SCHLESINGER, PRELUDE TO INDEPENDENCE: THE NEWSPAPER WAR ON BRITAIN, 1764–1776 (1958).
BARBARA J. SHAPIRO, "BEYOND REASONABLE DOUBT" AND "PROBABLE CAUSE" (1991).
BLACK'S LAW DICTIONARY (5th ed. 1979).
CATHERINE DRINKER BOWEN, THE LION AND THE THRONE: THE LIFE AND TIMES OF SIR EDWARD COKE (1956).
CHARLES MONTESQUIEU, THE SPIRIT OF THE LAWS (1748).
CHRISTOPHER HIBBERT, THE VIRGIN QUEEN: ELIZABETH I, GENIUS OF THE GOLDEN AGE (1992).
COLIN RHYS LOVELL, ENGLISH CONSTITUTIONAL AND LEGAL HISTORY (1962).

Daniel J. Kornstein, Kill All the Lawyers?: Shakespeare's Legal Appeal (1994).

Danny Danziger & John Gillingham, 1215: The Year of Magna Carta (2003).

Deuteronomy 19:18, 19.

Ecclesiastics 20:25.

Exodus 20:16.

Frederick G. Kempin Jr. Historical Introduction to Anglo-American Law (3d ed. 1990).

G. R. Elton, The Tudor Constitution (2d ed. 1982).

George Garnett, Law and Jurisdiction in the Middle Ages (1988).

Henry Wadsworth Longfellow, The Courtship of Miles Standish (1858).

J.G. Bellamy, The Criminal Trial in Later medieval England: Felony Before the Courts from Edward I to the Sixteen Century (1998).

J.H. Baker, An Introduction to English Legal History (2002).

J.M. Beattie, Crime and the Courts in England: 1660 – 1800 (1986).

J.R.R. Tolkien, Lord of the Rings (1954).

J. W. Ehrlich, The Holy Bible and the Law (1962).

John 8: 3-7.

John Ayto, Dictionary of Word Origins (1990).

John H. Wigmore, Evidence in Trials At Common Law § 2250 (McNaughton ed. 1961).

John Jay Osborn, Jr, The Paper Chase (1970).

Judges 7:16-22.

Kurt von S. Kynell, Saxon and Medieval Antecedents of the English Common Law (2000).

Leonard W. Levy, Origins of the Fifth Amendment: The Right Again Self-Incrimination (1968).

Lord Macaulay, The History of England (1979).

Luke 11:46 (King James).

Manual for Courts-Martial, United States (2008).

Nelson B. Lasson, The History and Development of the Fourth Amendment to the United States Constitution (1937).

Patricia M. Dugan, The Penal Process and the Protection of Rights in Canon Law (2005).

Proverbs 11:9.

R. Blain Andrus, Lawyer: A Brief 5,000 Year History (2009).

R.C. Van Caenegem, The Birth of the English Common Law (2d ed. 1988).

Rich Beyer, The Greatest Stories Never Told: 100 Tales from History to Astonish, Bewilder & Stupefy (2003).

Richard Brookhiser, What Would the Founders Do: Our Questions Their Answers (2006).

Robert R. Pearce, A History of the Inns of Court and Chancery (1848).

Roscoe Pound, The Development of Constitutional Guarantees of Liberty (1957).

Roscoe Pound, The Lawyer from Antiquity to Modern Times (1953).

S.E. Thorne, *The Early History of the Inns of Court with Special Reference to Gray's Inn*, Essays in English Legal History (1985).

Sadakat Kadri, The Trial: A History, from Socrates to O.J. Simpson (2005).

Samuel Dash, The Intruders: Unreasonable Searches and Seizures from King John to John Ashcroft (2004).

Susanna 1:164.

Susan Ford Wiltshire, Greece, Rome, and the Bill of Rights (1992).

T.S. Eliot, Murder in the Cathedral (1935).

The Columbia Encyclopedia (4th ed. 1975).

The Columbia Encyclopedia (4th ed. 1963).

The New Encyclopedia Britannica (15th ed. 2002).

The Oxford Classical Dictionary (1970).

The Works of Plato, *Apology* (Irwin Edman ed., Benjamin Jowett trans., Random House 1956).

Webster's New International Dictionary Of The English Language (2d ed. 1942).

Webster's Word Histories (1989).

Winston Churchill, A history of the English-Speaking Peoples, Vol. 1 (1958).

ARTICLES:

Alexander Volokh, *n Guilty Men*, 146 U. Penn. L. R.173 (1997).

A.W.B. Simpson, *The Early Constitution of the Inns of Court* 28 Cambridge L. J. 241 (1970).

Allen D. Boyer, *The Trial of Sir Walter Ralegh: The Law of Treason, The Trial of Treason and the Origins of the Confrontation Clause*, 74 Miss. L. J. 869 (2005).

Anthony Morano, *A Reexamination of the Development of the Reasonable Doubt Rule*, 55 B.U.L. Rev. 507 (1975).

Bruce P. Smith, *The Emergence of Public Prosecution in London, 1790-1850*, 18 Yale J. L. & Human. 29 (2006).

C.A. Morrison, *Some Features of the Roman and the English Law of Evidence*, 33 Tul. L. Rev. 577 (1958).

Charles Donahue, Jr., *Ius Commune, Canon Law, and Common Law in England*, 66 Tul. L. Rev. 1745 (1992).

Charles M. Gray, *Prohibitions and the Privilege Against Self-Incrimination*, in Tudor Rule and Revolution: Essays for G.R. Elton from His American Friends (Delloyd J. Guth & John W. McKenna eds., 1982).

Daniel Klerman, *Was the Jury Ever Self-Informing*, 77 S. Cal. L. Rev. 123 (2003-2004).

Daniel R. Coquillette, *The Legal Education of a Patriot: Josiah Quincy Jr.'s Law Commonplace (1763)*, 39 Ariz. St. L. J. 317 (2007).

Daniel Shaviro, *The Confrontation Clause Today in Light of Its Common Law Background*, 26 Val. U. L. Rev. 337 (1991).

David R. Stras, *Why Supreme Court Justices Should Ride Circuit Again*, 91 Minn. L. Rev. 1710 (2007).

Deborah A. Schwartz & Jay Wishingard, *The Eighth Amendment, Beccaria, and the Enlightenment: An Historical Justification for Weems v. United States Excessive Punishment Doctrine*, 24 Buff. L. Rev. 781 (1975).

Diana Woodhouse, *United Kingdom: The Constitutional Reform Act 2005 – Defending Judicial Independence the English Way*, 5 Int'l J. Const. L. 153 (2007).

Diane Parkin-Speer, *John Lilburne: a Revolutionary Interprets Statutes and Common Law Due Process*, 1 Law & Hist. Rev. 276 (1983).

Frank R. Herrmann, S.J. & Brownlow M. Speer, *Facing the Accuser: Ancient and Medieval Precursors of the Confrontation Clause*, 34 Va. J. Int'l. L. 481 (1994).

Fred O. Smith, Jr., *Crawford's Aftershock: Aligning the Regulation Of Nontestimonial Hearsay With The History And Purposes Of The Confrontation Clause,* 60 Stan. L. Rev. 1497 (2008).

George C. Thomas III, *History's Lesson for the Right to Counsel*, 2004 U. Ill. L. Rev. 543 (2004).

George Fisher, *The Jury's Rise as Lie Detector*, 107 Yale L.J. 575 (1997).

George Jarvis Thompson, *The Development of the Anglo-American Judicial System*, 17 Cornell L. Q. 9 (1932).

George Jarvis Thompson, *The Development of the Anglo-American Judicial System*, 17 Cornell L. Q. 395, 399 (1931-32).

George Jarvis Thompson, *The Development of the Anglo-American Judicial System*, 203, 209, *et seq*. (1932).

Harold J. Berman, *Religious Foundations of Law in the West: An Historical Perspective*, 1 J.L. & Religion 3 (1983).

Harold W. Wolfram, *John Lilburne: Democracy's Pillar of Fire*, 3 Syracuse L. Rev. 213 (1952).

J.H. Baker, *Cousellors and Barristers: An Historical Study*, 27 Cambridge L.J. 205 (1969).

J.M. Beattie, *Scales of Justice: Defense Counsel and the English Criminal Trial in the Eighteenth and Nineteenth Centuries*, 9 Law & Hist. 221 (1991).

Jacob Reynolds, *The Rule of Law and the Origins of the Bill of Attainder Clause*, 18 St. Thomas L. Rev. 177 (2006).

James A. Brundage, *The Medieval Advocate's Profession*, 6 Law & Hist. Rev. 439 (1988).

James Oldham, *Truth-Telling in the Eighteenth-Century English Courtroom*, 12 Law & Hist. Rev. 95 (1994).

James Robertson, *Quo Vadis, Habeas Corpus?*, 55 Buff. L. Rev. 1063 (2008).

Jeffrey K. Sawyer, *Benefit of Clergy in Maryland and Virginia*, 34 Am. J. Legal Hist. 49 (1990).

Joel N. Bodansky, *The Abolition of the Party-Witness Disqualification: An Historical Survey*, 70 Ky. L. J. 91 (1981-82).

John Langbein, *The Criminal Trial Before the Lawyers,* 45 U. Chi. L. Rev. 263 (1978).

John H. Langbein, *Shaping the Eighteenth-Century Criminal Trial: A View from the Ryder Sources*, 50 U.Chi. L. Rev. 1 (1983).

John H. Langbein, *The Historical Origins of the Privilege Against Self-incrimination at Common Law*, 92 Mich. L. Rev. 1047 (1994).

John H. Langbein, *The Origins of Public Prosecution at Common Law*, 17 Am. J. Legal Hist. 313 (1973).

John H. Langbein, *The Prosecutorial Origins of Defense Counsel in the Eighteenth Century: The Appearance of Solicitors*, 58 Camb. L. J. 314 (1999).

John H. Wigmore, *Required Numbers of Witnesses; A Brief History of the Numerical System in England*, 15 Harv. L. Rev. 83 (1901-02).

Justin C. Barnes, *Lessons from England's "Great Guardian of Liberty": A Comparative Study of English and American Civil Juries*, 3 U. St. Thomas 345 (2005).

Kenneth Graham, *Confrontation Stories: Raleigh on the Mayflower*, 3 Ohio St. J. Crim. L. 209 (2005).

Laura Ikins Stern, *Inquisition Procedure and Crime in Early Fifteenth-Century Florence*, 8 Law & Hist. Rev. 297 (1990).

Louis J. Sirico, Jr., *The Federalist and the Lessons of Rome*, 75 Miss. L. J. 431 (2006).

Martin R. Gardner, *The Mens Rea Enigma: Observations on the Role of Motive in the Criminal Law Past and Present*, 1993 UTAH L. REV. 635 (1993).

Michael MacNair, *Sir Jeffrey Gilbert and His Treatises*, 15 LEGAL HIST. 252 (1994).

P.R. Glazebrook, *The Making of English Criminal Law: The Reign of Mary Tudor*, 1977 CRIM. L.R. 582 (1977).

Paul Brand, *Courtroom and Schoolroom: the Education of Lawyers in England prior to 1400*, 60 BULL. INST. OF HIST. RESEARCH 147 (1987).

Paul M. Rashkind, *Gideon v. Wainwright: A 40th Birthday Celebration and the Threat of a Midlife Crisis*, THE FLORIDA BAR JOURNAL, March 2003, Volume 77: No. 3.

Peter Westen, *The Compulsory Process Clause*, 73 MICH. L. REV. 71 (1974).

Rafael Alberto Madan, *The Sign and Seal of Justice*, 7 AVE MARIA L. REV. 123 (2008).

Randolph N. Jonakait, *The Rise of the American Adversary System: America Before England*, 14 WIDENER L. REV. 323 (2009).

Richard Burst, *The 25 Greatest Legal Movies: Tales of Lawyers We've Loved and Loathed*, ABA JOURNAL August 2008.

Richard M. Fraher, *Conviction According to Conscience: The Medieval Jurists' Debate Concerning Judicial Discretion and the Law of Proof*, 7 LAW & HIST. R. 23 (1989).

Richard M. Fraher, *The Theoretical Justification for the New Criminal Law of the High Middle Ages: "Rei Publicae Interest, Ne Crimina Remaneant Impunita,"* 1984 U. ILL. L. REV. 577 (1984).

Robert Kry, *Confrontation Under the Marian Statutes: A Response to Professor Davies*, 72 BROOK. L. REV. 493 (2007).

Robert Popper, *History and Development of the Accused's Right to Testify*, 1962 WASH. U.L.Q. 454 (1962).

Robert Stein, *Rule Of Law: What Does It Mean?*, 18 MINN. J. INT'L L. 293 (2009).

Roger D. Groot, *The Jury in Private Criminal Prosecutions Before 1215*, 27 AM. J. LEGAL HIST. 113 (1983).

Scott D. Gerber, *The Court, the Constitution, and the History of Ideas,* 61 VAND. L. REV. 1067 (2008).

Seymour W. Warfel, *Quartering of Troops: The Unlitigated Third Amendment*, 21 TENN. L. REV. 723 (1951).

Sir Fredrick Pollock, *English Law Before the Norman Conquest*, 14 L. Q. REV. 291 (1898).

Stephan Landsman, *From Gilbert to Bentham: The Reconceptualization of Evidence Theory*, 36 WAYNE L. REV. 1149 (1990).

Stephan Landsman, *The Rise of the Contentious Spirit: Adversary Procedure in Eighteenth Century England*, 75 CORNELL L. REV. 497 (1990).

Steven G. Calabresi, *The Historical Origins of the Rule of Law in the American Constitutional Order*, 28 HARV. J. L. & PUB. POL'Y 273 (2005).

Susanna Frederick Fischer, *Playing Poohsticks with the British Constitution: The Blair Government's Proposal to Abolish the Lord Chancellor*, 24 PENN. ST. INT'L L. REV. 257 (2005).

Theodore Waldman, *Origins of the Legal Doctrine of Reasonable Doubt*, 20 J. HIST. OF IDEAS 299 (1959).

Thomas Davis, *What Did the Framers Know, and When Did They Know It? Fictional Originalism in Crawford v. Washington*, 71 BROOK. L. REV. 105 (2005).

Thomas A. Green, *The Jury and the English Law of Homicide, 1200-1600*, 74 MICH L. REV. 414 (1976).

W. Peter Westen, *The Compulsory Process Clause*, 73 MICH. L. REV. 71 (1974).

Walter Ullmann, *Medieval Principles of Evidence*, 62 THE LAW QUARTERLY REV. 77 (1946).

Walter Ullmann, *Some Medieval Principles of Criminal Procedure*, in JURISPRUDENCE IN THE MIDDLE AGES (1980).

William F. Duker, *English Origins of the Writ of Habeas Corpus: A Peculiar Path to Fame*, 53 N.Y.U. L. REV. 983 (1978).

William E. Nelson, *Authority and the Rule of Law in Early Virginia,* 29 OHIO N.U.L. REV. 305 (2003).

William E. Nelson, *Government by Judiciary: The Growth of Judicial Power in Colonial Pennsylvania,* 59 SMU L. REV. 3 (2006).

William E. Nelson, *The Utopian Legal Order of the Massachusetts Bay Colony, 1630-1686*, 47 AM. J. LEGAL HIST. 183 (2005).

MOVIES AND TV:

A FEW GOOD MEN (Columbia Pictures 1992).

A FUNNY THING HAPPENED ON THE WAY TO THE FORUM (United Artists 1966).

ANATOMY OF A MURDER (Columbia Pictures 1959).

BECKET (Paramount 1964).

BRAVEHEART (Paramount Pictures 1995).

COPS (Fox 1989-present).

Dog the Bounty Hunger (A&E 2004–present).

ELIZABETH (Gramercy 1998).

ELIZABETH: THE GOLDEN AGE (2008).

Frost/Nixon (Universal Studios 2008).

Gunsmoke (CBS 1952–61).

HISTORY OF THE WORLD, PART I (20th Century Fox 1981).

Judd, for the Defense (ABC 1967–1969).

JUDGMENT AT NUREMBERG (United Artists 1961).

KINGDOM OF HEAVEN (20th Century Fox 2005).

L.A. Law (NBC 1986–94).

Laugh-In (NBC 1968–73).

Law and Order (NBC 1990-present).

Matlock (NBC 1986–92).

MINORITY REPORT (DreamWorks and 20th Century Fox 2002).

MY COUSIN VINNY (20th Century Fox 1992).

Nancy Grace (HLN February 21, 2005 – present).

NATIONAL LAMPOON'S ANIMAL HOUSE (Universal Pictures 1978).

Owen Marshall: Counselor at Law(ABC 1971–1974).

Petrocelli's (NBC 1974–1976).

Perry Mason (CBS 1957–66).

PRESUMED INNOCENT (Warner Bros. 1990).

RESTORATION (Miramax 1995).

ROBIN HOOD (Buena Vista Pictures 1973).

Rumpole of the Bailey (BBC 1975–92).

SEVEN BRIDES FOR SEVEN BROTHERS (Metro-Goldwyn-Mayer 1954).

STAR WARS (20th Century Fox 1977).

THE ADVENTURES OF ROBIN HOOD (Warner Brothers 1938).

THE ADVOCATE (Europe = THE HOUR OF THE PIG) (1993).
The Bold Ones: The Lawyers (NBC 1968–1972).
THE COURTSHIP OF EDDIE'S FATHER (Metro-Goldwyn-Mayer 1963).
THE GODFATHER (Paramount Pictures 1972).
THE LIFE AND TIMES OF JUDGE ROY BEAN (Cinerama Releasing 1972).
THE LION IN WINTER (Universal Pictures 1968).
THE LORD OF THE RINGS (New Line Cinema 2001–2003).
THE PAPER CHASE (20th Century Fox 1973).
The Practice (20 Century Fox TV 1997–2004).
THE SAINT (Paramount Pictures 1997).
THE THREE MUSKETEERS (20th Century Fox 1973).
THE FOUR MUSKETEERS (20th Century Fox 1974).
THE VIRGIN QUEEN (20th Century Fox 1955).
THE WESTERNER (Samuel Goldwyn 1940).
TO KILL A MOCKINGBIRD (Universal Pictures 1962).
TOMBSTONE (Hollywood Pictures 1993).
V FOR VENDETTA (Warner Bros. 2006).
Wanted: Dead or Alive (CBS 1958–61).
WITNESS (Paramount Pictures 1985).
WITNESS FOR THE PROSECUTION (United Artists 1957).
YOUNG MR. LINCOLN (20th Century Fox 1939).

MISCELLANEOUS:

Boston Massacre Trial *available at* http://www.bostonmassacre.net/trial/index.htm (last visited 13 June 2007).

CRIMINAL TRIALS 389–520 (DAVID JARDINE ed., 1850) *available at* http://www.wfu.edu/~chesner/Evidence/Linked%20Files/Additional%20Assigned%20Readings/TRIAL%20OF%20SIR%20WALTER%20RALEIGH.htm (last visited 3 June 2007).

Doom (id Software 1993).

George Hodak, ABA Journal, March 2009.

Inner Temple Library at http://www.innertemplelibrary.org.uk/welcome.htm (last visited 15 May 2007).

MANUAL FOR COURTS-MARTIAL, UNITED STATES (2008).

Old Bailey *available at* http://www.oldbaileyonline.org.

Quintilian, http://www.thelatinlibrary.com/quintilian.html (last visited 7 July 2007).

Quintilian, http://www.public.iastate.edu/~honeyl/quintilian/index.html (last visited 7 July 2007).

THE CATHOLIC ENCYCLOPEDIA at http://www.newadvent.org/cathen/08256b.htm (last visited 7 July 2007).

THE CATHOLIC ENCYCLOPEDIA http://www.newadvent.org/cathen/11173c.htm (last visited 11 July 2007).

The State of Florida, Department of Corrections, http://www.dc.state.fl.us/oth/timeline/1963-1965.html (last visited 8 July 2007).

The Liberty Library of Constitutional Classics http://www.constitution.org/sr/lexrex.htm (last visited 5 December 2005).

Thomas Smith, *De Repvblica Anglorvm available at* http://www.constitution.org/eng/repang.htm (last visited 31 May 2007).

Printed in the USA
CPSIA information can be obtained
at www.ICGtesting.com
LVHW071543041023
760134LV00011B/246